I A

If your path led you within, would you continue?

-J. Kyle Short

Chapters

What are you producing?

"We are all self-made, but only the successful will admit it."

-Earl Nightingale

Where you are at in life is a direct result from choices that you have made. If you are financially secure, it is because you focused on a goal that you believed you needed to achieve, and you allowed nothing to stop you from attaining your goal. If you take great pride in the way your body looks, it is because you have worked diligently to be where you are. You created a vision of what or how you wanted your life to look and you did not stop until you were there. Some of us are still heading toward where we want to be. Some of us are still figuring it out. Some of us are still climbing our mountain, allowing it to become bigger with every step we take because we have a mentality of more (while often focusing on the lack).

How quickly is the raise you just obtained not enough? As we begin to earn more our cost of living increases. How often do we not even see an increase? We get a raise, buy a nicer car or home or things (that we believe increase happiness) and our savings in the bank is still 0. Or even worse, we buy that nicer home, give our children better things, buy our spouses that gift that sparkles more than the last, all while our spiritual or emotional bank is 0.

There is a scripture that says, "They will know you by your fruits." What fruit, to you, means more than any other? We typically excel in one or two areas in our lives while other areas suffer. And the areas that we are doing well are the ones we show off. These areas are the ones we take pride in. These are the areas in which we compete and compare with one another. These are the areas that we pretend are our only areas because they are the only ones we display. We pay little or no attention to the areas of need. But we are aware of these areas, aren't we? We just don't speak of them, and we absolutely don't let anyone see what we believe to be our deficit. We develop a pride in who we are because of our things and we believe this to be our identity. We begin to believe we are who we associate with, we are what we drive, we are the home we live in, we are the job title we have worked so hard to obtain, and we are our bank account. What happens when a goal gets in the way? What happens when our drive for achievement replaces our desire for fulfillment? We get burned out, fatigued, lost, stuck, feel as if the grass is greener elsewhere, and we doubt ourselves, our strengths and our abilities.

Again, I ask, what are you producing? Are you producing numbers? Income? Results for a company that would replace you if you dropped dead in a week. Which of your fruits are you nurturing and in what ways? Are they fruits that bring you fulfillment or are they fruits that are nice

to look at and tell people about? Are they things to
show off or things to behold? You pass on what you
produce to the ones who care about you the most.
When your time is said and done, and all the words
have been written in your book, what will be left?
What impact will you have contributed to the eyes
that look into yours? Do these eyes look into yours,
or do these eyes *look* for yours? I've spoken with
many people who have been given all the stuff
imaginable- cars, homes, money, material things,
vacations, name brands etceteras- all things able to
have been produced through the outcome of money,
wealth, and hard work. The common theme in
things that are "missing" from these people are
connections. Connections typically suffer when we
are what we do for a living.

I remember a Monday morning, tired, over-worked,
short-staffed, in which I attempted to insert my
house key into my office. I initially laughed, until
what I was doing sank in. As I thought about it,
questions started entering my mind. Was I spending
more time at work, producing results and income,
than I was at home producing a connection? Was I
simply providing things for my family to look at,
play with, touch, eat and eventually throw away?
What was the impact I was leaving? If I left the
world now, what would my children remember of
me? What would there be for them to hear about my
contribution to my family, loved ones, people with
whom I worked? What would they be told about

what I believe in and what evidence is there to support? Is there an abundance, or is there a lack? If I left the world today, what fruit would I leave to sustain my children and my family?

I remember speaking with a lady who was given all material things imaginable. I can still recall the way she stated, "My father gave me everything I ever asked him for. But all I ever wanted was a hug." The freest of gifts was the one withheld. The father in this story was doing what he believed to be the best option- providing financial support so that his family could enjoy a life of comfort. He had a goal as a child to be rich. And his goal was achieved. His goal required time away from his wife, and time away from his three children. It required hard work, long hours and he stated he didn't take a vacation for 16 years. He worked seven days a week. He missed dance recitals and football games. He missed important events in his children's lives. He missed building a connection with little eyes that looked for his. He was not only producing wealth; he was producing an impact.

In what ways are you producing your impact? Do not simply look for evidence you can see. Look for the unseen and the unspoken.

A woman throws a stone into a still pond and it creates ripples. The stone sinks to the bottom and is no longer able to be viewed. The ripples bring movement to a stick floating stagnantly atop the water. They cause reeds to move that are planted near the edge of the pond. The grass lining the small body of water is now dampened by the woman's stone, by her action. The water now makes room for the stone's presence. The stick will slowly lose momentum and remain stuck in the pond. It will eventually fail to remember the movement recently produced. The reeds have no option of relocating or doing more than they have been given to do- it appears as though they are impacted minimally, if at all. The grass will dry and forget about the stone and its ripples. But the pond is forever changed. It has been added to. It has been impacted.

Who are you in the story? What is your role? Are you possibly an unseen character? Perhaps you are a tree watching others impact those around you, believing you are not able, overlooking your own beauty and contribution. Or maybe you are the wind, gently touching everything in a subtle, noticeable way, while often going without recognition. Are you the bird flying overhead, looking down on everyone in this story, keeping your distance for fear of pain, rejection or failure? You are whatever role you choose to be. An impact, like the stone in this story, is relative. You may not notice the addition or influence you have on the pond (which is symbolic for any external thing that you have the ability to enhance). We do not always see the fruits that are produced from the seeds that we plant. But know this, everything that we do plants a seed. Every word that we speak. Every hand that we offer. Every look that we give. All of the love that we provide, and all of the love that we withhold. All seeds.

What we produce is a direct result of what we plant. So, pay attention to your seeds. They are thrown out in every single thing that we do.

This writing has a purpose. That purpose is to be determined by you. I cannot tell you what your purpose is; however, I can tell you what it is not. It is not to speed through. It is not to take lightly. It is not to stagnate or lose interest. It is not to finish quickly and move on to the next thing. It is not to give up. It is not to adapt or adopt someone else's purpose as your own. It is not to remain confused or disheartened. It is not to remain unaware. It is not to be lazy or gluttonous. It is not to be envious or bitter about what you do not have. It is not to let someone else do your work. It is not to be defined by another person. It is not to be codependent. It is not to be addicted. It is not to be forgotten or left out. It is not to fit in. It is not to be someone else's happiness.

My purpose may differ from yours, or ours may be shared. However, that does not mean that we will do it the same way. I cannot be you and you cannot be me and we cannot be another. I would fail at being you and vice versa. You are not your mother or your father. You are not your sister or your brother. You are not your priest or holy man. You do not need to be anyone, except you. The greatest and most beautiful thing you can be is you. If you are here, then you may have forgotten your own beauty. If you are here, then you may have forgotten your own truth. If you are here, you may have forgotten that failure gives birth to invention. I am here to remind you, that you are enough. You will always be enough. It is in your own voice that you read these words, and you may not believe your own voice. I am also here to show you how. It is your own path, not my own, that will get you to where you are going. If it is a new path, that means it is uncleared and may be difficult, as it should be. Things of benefit have a price. What price are you willing to pay? Are you willing to exchange your suffering for serenity? Are you willing to cross the bridge from darkness into self-love? Are you willing to fumble around in the mist and the rain and the fog to locate the door? If you are here, these answers are yes.

People often speak to me about waiting to hear from their Higher Power as if they are expecting the clouds to part. We overstep the stones on our path in search of the waterfall. Have we forgotten that the same one to make the water also made the stone? It is in our perception that we assign the falls more beauty than the stones. What is a foundation but a rock?

The Lotion Principle

If I don't have time to put lotion on after the shower, I will find an excuse to not do something even more productive that takes a longer amount of time. In reality, what does that take, 3 entire minutes? Not even one handful of minutes to give my skin what it needs. I will spend more than 3 minutes a day scratching an itch. Why not cluster it all together? There is no doubt I could find many handfuls of reasons to explain or excuse why I just don't have 3 minutes to take care of myself. I need to go to work. I need to get my project done (the one I have been doing on and off, mostly off, for 2 years). I need to make coffee. I need to eat. I need to get the grass cut. I need to make that phone call (the one I have been putting off for days, weeks or months, but suddenly it's monumentally more important than putting lotion on dry skin). I have e-mails to respond to. I "have" to do this. I "need" to do that. In this mental exhaustion, I am not saying what *is* important. I am saying what is *not* important: self-care.

Let's re-frame these thoughts. I am not as important as my job. I am not as important as that project (that I don't really like or enjoy). I am not as important as coffee. I am not as important as food. I am not as important as the grass growing in my yard. I am not as important as making the phone call I have been avoiding for too long that I can't even remember. I am not as important as an e-mail (that I don't really want to send). I am not important. This is the message that I am telling myself when I can't find the time (as though time was misplaced somehow) to put lotion on after the shower. The lotion is just an example. Input something you used to do, quickly, that you no longer "have the time" to do. What is the message you are secretly, subliminally telling yourself? Are you not worth moments of time? If I am not worth 3 minutes now, I will never be worth 5. If I don't give myself 3 minutes, will anyone else? If I overlook myself, won't others? How I treat myself is how I teach other people to treat me.

Let's start a new habit. One that uplifts. One that fulfills. A habit that can start the entire process of self-revitalization. Where you are going to begins today. It must begin right now. Forever is always and will always be right now. How will you begin your day? How will you end your day? We start these lists of things we want to do, be and accomplish, but do we finish? How much of this list do we complete? We get bored. We get tired. We get complacent. We get stagnant. We stop. We give in. We give up. Perhaps the list is too long. Are you starting with a goal that will take hours but can't find the minutes? Begin where it makes sense. Not at the end, but right here. The future is today. The future is this moment. What new routine can you begin that will only take a few minutes? Are you able to still your mind long enough to take a shower and find gratitude for your limbs and your joints? Or are you replaying that conversation that you had yesterday, last week or last year? The one that disturbs your sleep at night. The one that keeps you from disassembling your wall. The one that you project onto your loved ones. The one that you wear like a wound. Gratitude will heal you. Gratitude will heal your wound, but you must first find the minutes to allow for your healing. Are you able to wake up without hitting snooze and saying a prayer of thankfulness for being given another day? Each day is a day that we receive. We often get caught up in looking at the packaging and not the gift. We wake up and dread is what greets us. Our mind immediately begins racing with what we "have" to do today. All those meaningless chores. All the mundane tasks of life. Surely this is not our purpose. To be repetitive until we die. Are we not able to wake up, take a deep, fresh breath, and pay attention to the air in our lungs and exhale appreciation? Instead of hitting snooze, take those new sacred moments and express gratefulness for the things overlooked: the one laying next to you that you've forgotten to express love to, the children in their beds that you've not had the time to provide attention, the home that keeps you warm and safe at night, to the Creator that provided all this beauty in the world that you just don't have the time to view. But what about you? Do you dare to take these blessed moments and sit in your own beauty? Or are you too marred? Are you too imperfect? Is there something no one else knows that prevents you from realizing your own sacredness? Is it the wall? Is it the mentality of lack or not enough? What is it that has prevented you from realizing how Divine you are? What it is that keeps you from looking at your reflection? What is it that keeps you from forming a bond with the most precious of life- your own? Are you any less Divine than the wind that blows the trees?

On the next few pages, I am going to ask that you begin listing off descriptive words that you believe others would list about you (external). On another page, begin writing words that you would use as your own description (internal).

_____

_____

_____

_____

_____

_____

_____

_____

_____

_____

_____

_____

_____

_____

Are the two sections you filled out aligned? Are there words from the external list that you would like to change? Are you able? Are there words you want to keep, or even enhance? What about the internal list? Are there words you want to change? Are there words you want to amplify or add? Are you able? If you focus on how something can't be done, or why, you are right. If you believe you are able, change will occur. It is not the belief of possibility of change that is enough. It is the action behind the belief. If I believe I am worth spending time to put lotion on, I will do it. If not, I will not. What words do you want to become synonymous with your own name? The words on these lists that you most despise, when did these become commonplace? Once upon a time, you did not use these words to define or describe you. So why now? I understand using pain as a fuel to the fire, but do not mistake fuel for a shackle. If you choose to keep a "negative" word on a list, be sure to use it to benefit you, not to keep you from growth. Don't allow pain to keep you from fulfillment. Don't allow pain to keep you from destiny. Don't allow another minute, week or year go by with these old tapes reminding you of your faults. The tapes that used to scream at you but have become background noise, always running without a mute. These tapes that keep you from sleeping soundly. These tapes that you hate but don't know what you would do without. These tapes that you have used as a crutch to justify holding onto your pain. Will you let them go? Do you believe that you can? Don't give your sacred power away to what doesn't serve you or lift you. We all respond to the fear of rejection or inadequacy. When is that last time someone told you there is another way? Is it now?

Take a moment and feel what it would be like if you allowed love to embrace you. If you whispered the words, "I am enough," would you believe?

Close your eyes and take 3 deep exhales, but do not allow them to be without noise. Push out the stale energy, force out the things from the past that you want to release. Feel the old tapes leaving on your breath.

Take one more deep breath, but on this exhale, feel relief. Let it be likened to the first calmed breath after a marathon or the first caught breath after a sacred vow. Slow it down. Slacken your shoulders. Take your tongue off the roof of your mouth. Just be for a few moments. Exist, fully alive, in this space. You are worth the time.

What is it that you are here to do? Not in the building you are sitting or in the environment in which you are physically, but at this moment. While you are seated, what is it that you will do, right now, to change your life forever? Forever is now. Forever will always and only be right now. So, I ask again: What is it you are trying to do? Who is it you are trying to be? Bring your most important goal to the front of your mind. Make it your only vision. See it. Feel it. Believe the only outcome for this goal is the possibility. Believe the only outcome for this goal is an achievement. Envision yourself as having attained this goal. See yourself as light-hearted, freed from shame, unburdened from guilt. See yourself as having let go of all the lies that do not serve you, that never have sustained you. See that your wrists are no longer bound, and your feet as no longer bruised from walking in circles, down the same streets, in those same places where your dreams died. See where you are in this moment. Look down on yourself, in peace, with love. Feel what it means to have accomplished your most important goal. Feel that your freedom is now a choice. Feel that your freedom is now an opportunity. Feel that your freedom exists, in this very moment, in this very spot, in this sacred space. It is not the building that is sacred, it is you. It is what is within, not what is surrounding you. It is not your environment. It is not the light at the end of the tunnel because you are the light that is within the tunnel. Do not ever forget this Divine truth. You are the light. You are the achievement you have sought. You are the love that you search to find. You are enough. You have always been enough. You will always be enough.

I will ask you again: what is it that you came here, at this moment, to do?

If you whispered the words, "I am enough," would you believe?

Distractions

In the last chapter, I asked you to bring forward your most important goal, to make it your only vision. How many times have you pulled away from this goal by interruptions? I will now ask you to take a few moments (you are worth this time) and begin listing out what distracts you- use your notebook or the area provided on the next few pages. What typically adjusts your focus from what sustains, to what delays? Is it your phone? The constant texting and e-mail notifications. The group chats that you keep deleting yourself from only to be added into a new, less interesting one. Is it the people in your home? Is it television? What about the noise from the street or outside construction? Is your mind pulled away, or given away, by these outside influencers? Is it your pet asking you for attention or food or love? What external occurrences demand your peace? Is it the list of chores you don't want to do but suddenly find yourself interested in at least beginning (without finishing) one of the numbers on this never-ending list? What about our internal distractors? Am I finding myself caught up in my old tapes? Is my misplacement of focus due to past happenings that have left me wounded with shame or heavy with guilt? Is it that I'm wrapped up in future anxieties, worries or concerns? Or, is it the million-dollar question: Am I being distracted by fear?

I often tell my clients that I will not ask them to do something that I have not done myself. I believe the best experience is first-hand. I am a tactile learner and hands-on is the way in which I absorb information. However, I am not speaking about learning how to write an essay or studying the periodic table. I am talking about walking through the proverbial fire. What I speak of is what I know from doing. It is in the action of the deed, not the dream that will get you to where you want to be. It is the action of the deed, that will allow you to experience growth. However, there are times, in which we must grow through fire in order to learn how not to scald. Every one of these lists, I have done. Every one of these moments I ask you to face, I have faced. After all, it is the mirror that we avoid. It is the mirror that I have stared into. It is the face in the mirror, that I have offered my love and acceptance.

After you have completed your list, ask of each distraction, is this worth my time? What is it that I am exchanging for each interruption? Am I trading my peace for anxiety? Am I trading my comfort for abundance or the abundance that I have allowed myself to believe will make me happy or enough? Is responding to this text message worth giving up my momentum? Or will I stay fixated on my target?

We give in to our distractions because of the way in which we view our current action or goal. Go back to the Lotion Principle. When I give my mind away,

I am saying that what I am currently doing, what I am currently invested in, is not important enough for me to stay focused on. It is simply not important enough for me to maintain my line of thought and give my entire self to what I believe I want to accomplish. If this is true, why seek to complete? Am I attempting to find fulfillment through achievement? I am telling you right now, they are not the same. Not even close. How many of us have sought achievement, title, money, status, promotion, name-brand must-haves, a bigger house, a more beautiful spouse, better, better, better, only to find the void still exists? Is the void the distraction? Or, are you staying distracted to avoid the void? Give yourself a moment to reflect. Find your truth.

Now that you have your list of distractions, in what ways are you able to get through them? The quickest way is through, not around. What will you do now, at this moment, to get through? It must be more than silencing your phone. Put it in the other room. Create distance in between you, the goal and the nuisance. If you find yourself getting up and leaving your "project," then you were never invested, to begin with, and you would be better off to find another use of your time and interest. If you are going to listen to music, as I do when I create, find something peaceful, something stirring, without lyrics. The only words in this sacred space should come from within, not without. If there are people in your home that will not respect your need for quieted moments, remove yourself, politely, and find a spot in nature or somewhere you can ground yourself (which we will do together in a guided meditation at the end of this and every chapter). If you simply cannot get away from the distractions, don't allow anger to get you further off your path. Be gentle. Be kind. After all, it's not about the distraction, it's about your perception of the distraction. It is your mind that has become accustomed to getting off course. Any negative emotion tied to an outside distractor is fueled by something you can't tolerate within. Many wise thinkers have likened all relationships to mirrors. It may also be said about outside events. We all have preferences, as we should. It is that which stings us that I am referencing. It is the thorn in the heart that Michael A. Singer speaks of in The Untethered Soul. The goal, in my opinion, is not to get around discomfort- it is to get through.

Take a moment and feel what it would be like if you allowed love to embrace you. If you whispered the words, "I am enough," would you believe?

You may have left a noisy environment, filled with chaos and stress to find yourself at this moment. Being grounded means staying present despite interference. Grounding is learning to channel energy and focus to work for you, not against you. It is allowing your thoughts to be there without opposition. It may involve visualization; seeing your issues, problems, obstacles, thoughts and/or fears and allowing them to exist without a fight. It is seeing them drift away from you. It is allowing yourself to be released from the anchor and setting sail. Now begins our next practice...

Close your eyes and take 3 deep exhales, but do not allow them to be without noise. Push out the stale energy, force out the things from the past that you want to release. Feel the old tapes leaving on your breath.

Take one more deep breath, but on this exhale, feel relief. Let it be likened to the first calmed breath after a marathon or the first caught breath after a sacred vow. Slow it down. Slacken your shoulders. Take your tongue off the roof of your mouth. Just be for a few moments. Exist, fully alive, in this space. You are worth the time.

What is it that pulls you away from your goal? What is it that takes your clarity? What is it that you want to no longer hold and no longer be held by? Bring it to your mind. Give it form. If it is a fear, you may see it as a stone or any other object of your selection. Perhaps you have multiple "forms" you are releasing. You can insert them onto the leaves of an old oak tree hanging over a slow streaming river. With each inhale, see the tree move as if your breath is the wind. On the exhale, allow a leaf to fall into the river. What distraction does this leaf represent? Do you see it flowing away from you? Do you see it winding downstream and slowly drifting out of sight? Do you feel relief from the distance now created in your mind and this obstacle? Is your leaf an emotion that no longer serves you? What is the next leaf that will fall? On the next inhale, do you see the movement and sway of the tree? Do you feel the sunlight dancing around the limber branches? Can you feel the warm embrace of sunlight on your face? Can you feel the wind dances around you as you are seated, peacefully, on the bank of this river? Do you see this tree as fully alive even as it sheds the leaves of its old self? What is the next leaf to fall? Are you able to release that which no longer serves you but interferes with your peace? How willing are you to come to this sacred space, time and time again to find yourself one with all that surrounds you? Will you sit in this moment until the only leaves that remain are not distractors but reminders of how necessary you are? Will you sit with me in this space and allow love to transform your every cell? Will you sit within yourself and step out of your mind and into your heart? Will you allow yourself the moments of time to heal what you once thought broken?

If you whispered the words, "I am enough," would you believe?

The Problem with Goals

I wonder what your thoughts were on reading the title of this chapter. Did you jump to the conclusion that I am saying goals are a "bad" thing? How far into your internal dialogue did you travel? Or did you simply move forward?

We spend days, weeks, months, years and sometimes even decades attempting to achieve a goal only to be dissatisfied upon completion. We spend very little time acknowledging or celebrating our accomplishments. We climb the mountain, take a breath, look around and see a slightly taller mountain in the distance. Perhaps immediately we become disheartened that we are not on the crest of the *other* mountain. We begin comparing our current foundation with the one that appears more beautiful in the distance. If I could just get *there*, then I'll be happy. The view must be incredible from over *there*. I bet I can see even more glorious heights from that one. How many can relate to what I'm conveying? In the previous chapter, I referred to confusing achievement with fulfillment. Are we basing our happiness on a goal? It doesn't work that way. Eckhart Tolle said, "Happiness depends on conditions being perceived as positive, inner peace does not." The mountain (goal) does not determine my happiness. My happiness is based upon the way in which I view the mountain. My happiness is based on the way in which I view all things. I love my job. I obtain fulfillment through the work I am able to do. I believe it to be my calling. That does not mean that I don't get frustrated when the internet goes down or when a client just will not listen to my expert, sage advice. After all, I know best. Right? My way is *the* way. Right? Obstacles are a nuisance and must be gotten rid of in order for me to progress and find happiness. Right?

Wrong.

The obstacle is not the issue. The issue is my perception. The fault exists within my mind. It is in those old tapes that tell me how life must be lived in order to be happy. To have that white picket fence with 2.5 children, to live in a cul-de-sac, have cookouts with the neighbors and exchange one-ups and better than's, to show off the newest brand name must-have, that's the goal, right? To have the relationship with your neighbor where you greet them with a smile while subliminally telling them you are slightly better, then shutting the door and telling your spouse, "Can you believe them? Who do they think they are? Did you see the way blah blah blah?" That's the goal, right? To be on top, looking down at those closest. "That's not what I'm doing." Or is it?

Your stuff does not define you. It will all spoil.

We finally get to that plateau and immediately, without effort (because we are now conditioned to think this way), we find a flaw in the picture. We begin focusing on what we don't like. We see what is "wrong." We see the slight color variation on the wall in our new office. We see the edge of the new desk that is worn. We see a stain on the couch from where the sunlight has been hitting it for years. We can hear the noise from the neighbor in the cul-de-sac that we just *had* to move in to. And it's terrible. "Can you believe it?! You'll never guess…"

If we are able to notice we are noticing, that's a huge step. Pay attention to your dialogue. Write it out. Recall to memory the last minor thing that upset you. I am not talking about death or loss. I'm talking about the traffic jam you were in earlier. I'm referencing the conversation you had last night when your significant other said the *wrong* word. What was the dialogue like in your mind? Write it out. Look at it. Give it form.

_____

_____

_____

_____

_____

_____

_____

_____

_____

_____

_____

_____

When we take a step back, we are now able to see our real problem, our true obstacle: our perception. Not collective, but individual. Or, is your perception based upon what others have told you to believe or feel? Do you vote for something just because your loved ones do? Do you believe in a cause without having asked, "Do I really care about this?" Are you blinding following? Are you blindly leading? Have I spent the years of my life thinking about what I want, or what others want? How many times have we heard someone say, "You should do ____," or "Why can't you just see it my way?" Are you not allowed to have your own set of eyes? Are you not permitted to embrace your own set of ideals? Have you ever asked yourself the questions in this book? Let me remind you, you are worth this time. Do you even want that promotion? Is the money worth the time away from your children? Are you seeking to fill the void that no thing can? More stuff will not complete you.

Years ago, I had a friend who got his business degree. He quickly realized he did not like the doors this opened for him. He did not feel comfortable in the environments in which he was placed. He continued working fast food and eventually joined the armed forces. He was following (blindly) the encouragements (probably forced) of what he *should* do. He was a young man, being told by an older man, how to live *his* life. Have you ever misread a recipe and created something inedible?

Or, are you like me and have had the experience of following a recipe to the letter only to find what you created to be unpalatable? All the time spent, the ingredients, the money, wasted, right?

A lesson does not create waste.

I am in no way saying to change your career or switch positions to something more "fun." What I am saying is to find a new way to re-engage. Rediscover your passions. I have spent many years in the chemical addiction field. There is a term that every counselor/therapist/physician/teacher is aware of: compassion fatigue- getting burned out on helping others. What we spent years learning to do, we want to give up. I know many highly trained, expertly skilled therapists who have simply walked away. We get bogged down with clinical work, not the face-to-face client interaction, but the behind the scenes work. The documenting, the case notes, the emotional toll, the laying in bed at night wondering if you are making an impact. Is it worth it to keep going?

OF COURSE!

If you once found fulfillment in your career, I would say to you it wasn't the career that changed, the way in which you view it has. Do I want to write a book, or do I want to have written a book? If you find yourself getting bored, then your heart is not in it. Re-discover. Re-connect. Re-engage.

If you want to change, change. There is no one stopping you. You can list reasons as to why you *must* continue doing what you are grudgingly doing… but they are just excuses. You are co-signing them. My excuses are not for you; they are for me. They are so I can stay safe and stagnant inside my comfort zone. I can stay stuck and justify staying stuck because "it's what everyone does."

Dare to show yourself. Be seen. You are worth this time.

Is what we seek our truth?

Is it necessary?

Does it improve upon my fulfillment?

If you whispered the words, "I am enough," would you believe?

Close your eyes and take 3 deep exhales, but do not allow them to be without noise. Push out the stale energy, force out the things from the past that you want to release. Feel the old tapes leaving on your breath.

Take one more deep breath, but on this exhale, feel relief. Let it be likened to the first calmed breath after a marathon or the first caught breath after a sacred vow. Slow it down. Slacken your shoulders. Take your tongue off the roof of your mouth. Just be for a few moments. Exist, fully alive, in this space. You are worth the time.

Bring to your mind a few of your most recent goals. Envision goals that have been achieved and goals that you are currently working on. Feel what it felt like to have overcome the obstacles that stood in your way when you set out to accomplish these goals. Remember what you felt when you set out to complete the goal in which you are currently focused on. Are these goals your own or do they belong to someone else? Do they belong to someone who isn't beside you now? Were they input, or were they implant? Is this a path you truly desire, in your heart, to continue walking? What is it you wish you achieve from this goal? Is it out of fear that you walk this path? Is it out of scarcity that you call out for something greater? A thing born in fear will reproduce an offspring of fear. This is the cycle that we seek to break at this moment. It is here, in this sacred space, that we seek to undo what no longer serves us. It is here that we ask: What do I want?

How much time have you spent asking this question? What do you, the individual hearing or reading these words, want? Do not force a response. Allow the answer to come to you. Sit within yourself, repeating this question. What do I want? What do I want? Now ask, why do I want? Do you want more in order to give? You can give from where you are. You can give what you have.

What is it that you can give, non-material, in this moment?

Many people do not know how to answer the question, "What do I want?" Some say fear of selfishness overcomes them. Others fear of neglect overtakes them and tells them that they are not being grateful for what they have already. Release the judgments. You are not on trial. You are not the jury. You are not condemned. You have a right to respond. You have a duty to respond. No one can answer except you. No one has the right to respond to your questions. They are yours, and yours alone. We may share an answer, but we have different equations, we have different variables.

Recall moments of unfulfillment after having achieved a goal. What was missing? Was it an emotion? Was it joy? Was it a congratulation from another being? Was it recognition? If I don't recognize myself, how can another? If I don't acknowledge the beauty from where I stand, I will never see the beauty from another position. Things cannot be brighter in the future if they are not brighter in the present. We may need to open our eyes wider or step back from the details of the picture to see the entirety.

What have I been seeking? Am I looking outside for something that can only come from within? Do not discount the importance of your voice. It is your voice that you will listen to most often. You will accept your words over another's. Use them to identify. Use them to fulfill. Use them to re-establish, re-connect and re-discover. You are worth the time.

If you whispered the words, "I am enough," would you believe?

Who is This About?

If you've made it this far, I want to congratulate you. I've lost count of how many times I have given someone the opportunity (homework, task, a chore-depending upon the viewpoint) to begin internal work and then never hear from the person again. I've loaned the book The Power of Now to handfuls of clients who have left treatment prematurely. And every time a client left, the book has left with them as well. So, I buy another copy. The way I see it is that the message is there, and it travels with the person. I do not feel slighted or stolen from because I choose another way. Perhaps the message within is too uncomfortable (because love is uncomfortable to pain). Perhaps the message challenges the bricks of the wall, each with their own name, asking that the wall be dismantled. Perhaps that person is simply not ready at that time to look at the mirror and see the one that truly matters. Perhaps the beauty of the internal is beginning to surface and the person refuses to accept the beauty that exists. Most likely due to the scars, or faults, or flaws or _____ insert whatever word prevents you from acknowledging what is clear to others, what is so plainly viewed from loved ones that you refuse to receive. Whatever word you choose, it has a past derivative. And you are allowing it to take away from the present. This chapter asks what has been previously asked. Who is this really about? The goals that you have identified, who are they about?

Are they purposed from within, or from without? Do you seek to follow the footsteps of another "successful" person, perhaps a mother or a father that instructed (or forced their opinion on) you on how to be achievement-oriented, pay bills, own stuff, look the part, and do as you're told because "that's what people do?" Take a moment to identify yourself in the following quote…

"People are often unreasonable, irrational, and self-centered. Forgive them anyway. If you are kind, people may accuse you of selfish, ulterior motives. Be kind anyway. If you are successful, you will win some unfaithful friends and some genuine enemies. Succeed anyway. If you are honest and sincere people may deceive you. Be honest and sincere anyway. What you spend years creating, others could destroy overnight. Create anyway. If you find serenity and happiness, some may be jealous. Be happy anyway. The good you do today will often be forgotten. Do good anyway. Give the best you have, and it will never be enough. Give your best anyway. In the final analysis, it is between you and God. It was never between you and them anyway."

-Mother Teresa

How did this speak to you? What did it say? Take a moment to reflect on your goals. Are you your goals for you? Are they for another? What is it that you truly want? Have you found an answer to this question, yet?

We all want acceptance. We all fear rejection. Is it difficult for you to speak love while looking into the eyes of your partner? Do you break eye contact out of fear of being exposed? If there is discomfort, there is a reason for discomfort. If you can't look into their eyes, it's not about them. It is about you.

The things in which you attempt to reach… why? What is the meaning? What is the goal of the goal? You get this thing, and then what? You feel this emotion, and then what? Onto the next thing? Find a replacement for that which we just obtained? The internal garage sale. Out with the old, in with the soon to be old. What is the point? What is your point? Do you have one, or have you yet to find the point?

I am reminded of a client of the past. This person was struggling with feeling a purpose. This person felt he had "lost (his) edge." He had forgotten that he *is* that edge. I reminded him the time at present was a refurbishing, a clay pot in the kiln; an upgrade. He quickly smiled because he felt what I was telling him like water to his parched soul. He remembered this truth. He remembered his truth. He recalled events that led him to be where he was stationed in life. His physical location was a treatment facility; however, his spiritual location was on another level. It was beyond what we can perceive with our eyes. He remembered, at that moment, that his edge was not lost, because he was not lost. He was on his path.

Our paths are filled with beauty, and heartbreak, and laughter, and darkness, and cliffs and waterfalls. They are filled with twists and turns, inclines and straightaways, warm moments and moments of chill. Life. And death. There are beginnings and there are endings. All with their own purpose. I am not here to tell you what they are. But you have the ability to see the meaning for yourself. After all, you are the one that defines it. Being cynical and skeptical is a choice.

Are you on your own path, or are you on a path that was created by another? Are you sitting at a desk, unfulfilled because you're "supposed to?" Are you wearing the worn-out, lifeless shoes that belong to someone else? Wherever you are, are you there because you have chosen to be there? Is your destination one that you hand-picked? Have you made friends with your discomfort? Have you stayed in place because it's too difficult to do something else? How tired are you? Are you tired enough to lay down, or tired enough to do something about it?

∞

Take a moment and get your body settled into a comfortable position. Allow your spine to lift you while your shoulders relax. Take your tongue off the roof of your mouth. Inhale 3 deep breaths, paying attention to the expanse of your lungs. On each exhale, rid your body of old energy and stored emotions. Feel the past expectations that you want to let go of leaving your mind. Feel the expanse of freedom in each exhale. On the fourth exhale, sigh with relief.

Allow yourself to begin picturing where you are most comfortable. Perhaps it is laying on a warm, red-sand beach or a mountainous cabin surrounded by mossy oaks. Maybe it is watching a sunset with your most sacred connection. Or is it in your home at the time in which it feels most welcoming? Wherever it is, be there. Exist there. There is here. Marry this thought.

Where you are is of your choosing. No one led or forced you to be in this location. How did you get there? On your free will. Your heart led you. Your heart knows your greatest comfort, but your mind gets in the way. Your mind tells you what you "need" to do, or what is "best." This can oftentimes be highly inaccurate. Who is to say where you should be but you? Are you the author of your story or just the illustrator? Do you even have a credit in your book? Are you going to allow another author to write your story? To edit out the most intricate of details. To copy and paste their story into your own. To remember and misremember, to speak and misspeak, to tell and un-tell what makes you, you...

Or is it the thorn in your heart that has your voice? Perhaps this thorn creates a fear of becoming vulnerable and opening up to scrutiny and judgment from another. Or maybe your thorn was born from rejection or abandon. Maybe this thorn speaks on your inadequacies and failures. Does your thorn tell you of the strength you lack or your inability to achieve? Which voice do you allow to speak? Is there a voice you wish to regain control?

If you are comfortable, place your hand over your heart, or imagine doing so. Feel the area of the wound. Imagine a healing light coming from your hand to the place of infliction. Say to yourself, it is my love that I seek. My love is my purpose. It is my story that I create. Now remove your thorn. It is time, dear one.

When you remove the thorn, you will create a fresh wound. Perhaps the area around the thorn is scarred and hardened. Removing the thorn will produce fresh pain, but it will not infect. Your thorn is born of the past. The past is over. Let it remain over.

In the environment of your choosing, see the pen that is in your hand. See that cover of your book to be one that you selected. Watch as you write, with confidence, pen in one hand, the thorn in the other, the next page of your story. You are the author; you are the editor and you are the publisher. You chose who gets the privilege of hearing or reading your story. Because that's what it is, a privilege. If any person makes you feel as though it is anything other than an honor to hear your story, they are not your support. It is better you uncover this truth now than on the last page. Love mirrors love and light mirrors light. You are the love in your story, not another. You are the light in your story, not another. Your light can be amplified or enhanced by another, but it does not derive from another. You are that source.

If you wrote the words, "I am enough," would you believe?

If You Like Me, I'll Like Me

We learn through repetition. Some of the chapters may seem to overlap. It is intentional. The basis of this entire manual is to understand that you (I) are (am) enough. However, we need convincing to get there. Today I had an interaction with a woman who was telling me all the reasons in which she determined herself to be "inadequate." A title that I have identified within myself for more years than not. She went on to discuss the length and depth in which she cleans her home, the dishes, and the laundry and the meticulousness of every task. There are 6 mouths in that home, and she does the lion share of housework. She referred to the moment where you finally get "done" or at least to a point in which you can sit down, rest and breathe a sigh of relief only to find one more thing (there will always be at least one more thing) that "needs" to be done. The process starts all over.

I asked her, "Who are you trying to impress?"

She laughed and said, "I don't know."

I inquired, "Is it yourself?"

There was a pause. She smiled before stating, "Well, the kids don't seem to care what the house looks like!" I asked if she is willing to do internal work to the same degree in which she does external (house) work. I reminded her that the internal work is what will sustain her. It is what will help heal her.

She acknowledged being "very, very ready" to begin this work. I highlighted storms that will come. I spoke of days in which motivation will simply not be there. I also told her that all motivation is self-created. It is not an event that creates motivation. It is not pain or success. It is not money. It is not even lacking. It is the way in which all of these things are viewed.

It is not about what you do, it is about how you do it. It is not about what you say, it is about how you say it.

All motivation is self-created. Learn this now. Discipline may be what inspires motivation. And the discipline is merely doing. It is repeating. All of our lives, we spend repeating. For some illusionary reason, we are "fine" with repeating what ails us. We can tell our co-workers about all our problems at home (excluding ourselves from these stories), we can tell of our issues at work (excluding our roles in these issues or what we can do about them), and all of our issues in all of our relationships (excluding ourselves from these matters). We repeat our problems. We discuss, in-depth, our turmoil. But we can't find time to go to church or go to the gym or meditate or pray. We can find time to go to AA or NA, or Alanon or Naranon. We can't find time to go to Celebrate Recovery. We can't find time to go to a therapist or talk about what really ails us: US! We don't want to do what helps us because it gives us an excuse to stay stuck. It gives us a reason to keep clinging to our poison (alcohol, drugs, abusive relationships, jobs we hate, people who don't deserve our time, self-loathing/pity, anger, depression, anxiety, etc.). Without a good excuse, people will expect me to progress. What if I fail?

What if I succeed? What if I not only succeed, but I have fun doing so?!

I often ask clients to respond to the question: Why will I succeed? It is on computer paper and the remainder is completely blank. Rarely do people need another sheet of paper. I then ask those who feel comfortable doing so to read the paper out loud. Then I challenge those who don't want to read, to step out of their comfort zones. After they are read or kept quiet, I ask the group members, "How many of you would have had a longer response if the question was 'Why will I fail?'" It is always the majority that identify they know more about their scars than their strengths. It is because of the stories we repeat. People get bored with repetition, but we do it every single day. Often every single moment.

The average person has 60,000 thoughts in a day. How many of those thoughts are new thoughts? 5%? 10%? Pay attention. Notice your patterns. See your repetition. Know that you are the only one who can bring change to your path. At any point in your journey, you are able to go off-course. Will you dare to step away from what is familiar? Will you dare to step away from your pain and into the warmth of the sunlight? Are you going to determine yourself to be worth breaking that co-dependent relationship? The one with the man who doesn't care about your thoughts or the one with the woman who wants you to stay stuck so that she doesn't have to progress… You have your own story. These two are mine. How many thoughts do we have that do not serve us? Are these damaging thoughts our own, or have they been told to us? There are times that I believe the root to be most important. However, you can take a plant that is dying, introduce healthy soil, and that plant will not only thrive, but it will also reproduce healthy offspring. You are the plant. Your thoughts are the soil. I am terribly sorry for your wounds. I am sorry for the things you did not deserve, but you no longer have to take it or be responsible for the pain that was inflicted upon you. Choose today. Choose now. There is only ever now. Do not let it pass you by.

As with our goals, if we are seeking another person, of thing to fill our void or to create joy, it will not last. That person or title or thing will anger you, it will sadden you or it will end and there goes your happiness right along with it. If this is the case, then you were never truly joyous. It was an illusion. Happiness is based upon the way I view things happening around me. Joy comes from within. How many of you have fallen madly, passionately in love and have disregarded what other people have had to say? How many have fallen desperately in love despite seeing red flags or hearing warning sirens? How many have grown to detest that person that came to your mind? What, or in this scenario, who brought love now brings pain. Who once brought us freedom, now puts a lid on our box. Support becomes an imbalance. Addition becomes subtraction. When we determine who we are through another person, we fall. People can add to us. Things can amplify us. But they must not determine us. Stop waiting on someone to love you before you love yourself. Everything of worth comes from the beholder. What is a diamond but a former piece of coal? What is a piece of coal but a future diamond?

Take some time to write out your recurrent thoughts. Highlight the ones you want to keep. Star the ones you want to remove. Do it however you want to do it. This is for you. It is not for me. It is for no other.

_____

_____

_____

_____

_____

_____

_____

_____

The Internal

ME

Values

Morals

Beliefs

Principles

Character

Faith

Etc.

The External

OTHER

Titles

Family, friends, spouse

Relationships

Status, Bank Account

Stuff, notoriety

The way I am viewed

Etc.

my identity is then CREATED...

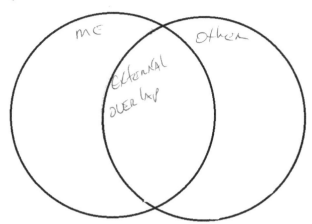

All things External CAN be removed,
taken Away, Divorced, lost, etc.
when this occurs...

I then Question my self-worth
Due to A "loss of identity." → Who Am I
                                    Now?

In this sacred space, in these sacred moments,
remember your extreme worth. Once upon a time
you knew. Remind yourself, beloved one, of your
supreme value. Do not allow another to speak for
you. Find your words. Use them now.

Imagine a young, withering sapling, hidden in the
shade of an older, more established tree, being
blocked from sunlight, and being neglected by the
soil. Can you feel the needs of this sapling? Will
you allow yourself to feel connected to it? See your
hands digging in the dirt, carefully taking this
young tree and planting it in the sunlight. Give
water to this young plant. See the wind sway it.
Watch the leaves turn up to the sun. Hear the rain
dropping around this little life that you helped
foster. Imagine a time-lapse. Watch this sapling
grow. See its limbs being created, formed and
extended. Watch as it climbs to new elevations,
providing shade to all surrounding. See the
necessity of this being. See the Divinity that created
this life. Where you already aware that you are this
tree? Are you aware that storms are necessary for
growth and expanse? Do you see all seasons as
needed, the cold and the warmth alike? Do you see
that the light makes way for the night and the night
breaks for the day? How much more important are
you than a tree? For a moment, you felt connected.
You felt responsible. You felt love for this life. You
are this life. It only takes moments to see yourself in
a new light. All you have to do is close the eyes that

look at you as undeserving. All you have to do is remove the words from repetition that do not serve you.

Words can heal. Words can bring life. Words can take life away. What will you do differently or in a new way with your words? Will you replant? Or will you wait on another to move you to another location? The only person who can love you the way you need to be loved is you. It has always been you. It will always be you.

If you spoke the words, "I am enough," would you believe?

The Anchor is the Sail

"What you can't accept, you will oppose, and in that opposition will be your bondage."

-Paul Ferrini

The above statement is saying that it is not the occurrence or situation that binds us, it is our opposition to the occurrence. We cannot move through fear by being unwilling to accept it. We move through fear by taking action. It is not simply hope that will change our outcome. I remember clinging to hope and if it were a lifejacket, and there are times it may have been. A lifejacket will not get you out of the water or off a stormy sea. A lifejacket will not feed you or keep you warm. Action is what will move you and get you to where you desire to be. But what is action without a plan? I cannot see a sunset by running east. What has been preventing you from taking action? What do you fear will result in taking action? Is this fear greater than the anticipated outcome? Take an action, but don't run out blindly into the road or set out to sea if a storm is coming. Find out what you like and find out what you don't like. Use failing and falling as a sail, not as an anchor.

I had a client who repeatedly referred to herself as being "on a boat in the middle of the ocean." One day I asked her if she enjoyed sailing, to which she replied she did. I then inquired as to why she uses being "on a boat in the middle of the ocean" if she enjoys being there. She replied, "Because I don't know where I'm going." I asked her if she is attempting to control her course or destination in this analogy. She stated, "Yes." I then asked, "Are you safe in this boat?" She replied, "Yes." I finally questioned, "What is wrong with putting the sail up and throwing the oars overboard? Can you let the wind be your Higher Power? What if you are trying to get somewhere you are not supposed to be?" It was as if something inside her changed from that moment on. She was still "on a boat in the middle of the ocean" but the way she looked at it was altered. She was refreshed and finally able to feel the sun and enjoy the wind.

During times of trial, I remember this conversation. I see myself as attempting to paddle a boat to a destination that does not serve me. I envision throwing my oars overboard and putting up the sail. I do not create the wind, but the One who does will guide me. In these times, I must accept my fear and my judgments. I accept my irrationality and pain. By doing so, I accept my love. We cannot move through pain by being unwilling to accept it.

I do not believe life is about trading in your cards for a new hand. I believe it is about learning when and how to best play your cards.

Our stories teach us and allow us to teach and assist others. Dishonesty can teach us honesty. Pride can teach us humility. Ignorance can teach us

acceptance and so on. However, if I am not willing
to learn, I will continue to mistake mud for
quicksand. What we don't like teaches us what we
enjoy, but only when we stop fighting.

In June of 2018, I deeply cut my middle right
finger. It was on the bend and in a very awkward
place. I'm sure stitches would have been given, had
I gone to the hospital. My lack of going is not the
point. In this wound, I was able to find vast
appreciation for my other unwounded digits. I wrote
about it that night so that I could remind myself to
stop overlooking what is simple and profound. I
have repeatedly overlooked many blessings, such as
having fingers that all work. Were it not for this
injury, I would continue to bypass the depth of what
I have been given.

Our greatest anchor is pain. And we all fear pain. I
have found that the bigger the ego, the bigger the
fear. The bigger the wall, the more frightened the
wounded child within. It is okay to acknowledge
your fear. It will actually begin to lessen when you
admit it. Try it out. I dare you. Admit a fear to
someone who is close to you, to someone who will
accept you no matter what. Will you be surprised
when they admit they have the same fear, or a fear
closely likened? We oftentimes try to shut the door
on the past and pretend it isn't there. Yet, at the
same time, we are plagued by the past and can't
seem to leave it alone. It is like walking through
filth, creating a mess in the house and pretending it

isn't there. And everyone else in the house pretends right along because of fear. "I don't want to make her mad," or "I don't know how to bring it up to him, so I don't." Not knowing how to do something doesn't get you off the hook from not doing it. Take action. Write down the things you want to say. Go back over them and edit. Take the emotions out of it if they will further the harm. Now speak. You deserve it. They deserve it. How much longer will you let fear prevent you from enjoying your journey? Will you get to your destination and be angry? Will you arrive and find a fault? Or will you set sail and allow life to continue to unfold. It's going to either way. Sometimes it rains and sometimes it hails. Your fear and your anger will not stop any of it.

My father didn't enter my life until I was 22. I remember wanting to be a front-page athlete in high school so that he would see the article and realize how great I am. It was through him that I was searching for my acceptance. (Of course, at the time, I did not know this). I wanted him to be proud of me. Or maybe I wanted him to come to a game and claim me. Or perhaps I wanted him to regret his absence and share my pain in the "lack of a role model." Or maybe…. You fill in the blank with your own experience. I know that whatever I reason I had for being front-page, it was out of lack, specifically lack of love. But love didn't originate at the source (the self). When love doesn't begin with me, it cannot be given to me. If I don't have self-love, you cannot love me properly. All the abundance from another will not fill that hole. It will always feel conditional. It will always be interpreted or misinterpreted. I will always find some type of fault in the other's love. I will always find fault with myself believe I am not worthy of that love, and I will project all of this fear onto the other. I will shift blame and point a finger at their reflection because looking at my own would be too painful. Something I cannot handle (because I believe I cannot handle it). If you focus on how something can't be done, then it can't. The absence of love taught me about the presence of love, but this lesson was not learned overnight. As a matter of fact, it took years. And every single step has worth. Go through the night. The sun will always rise.

In the Big Book, page 124, it states, "Showing others who suffer how we were given help is the very thing which makes life seem so worthwhile to us now... The dark past is the greatest possession you have. With it, you can avert death and misery for them."

Begin listing your barriers. Write out the things you are afraid to face. Make a note of the things that have prevented you from setting sail. Do not judge the content. Only write. If it is there, allow it to be there and put it down. Are there things in your life, situations, occurrences, scars, obstacles that you do not believe you can or have not been able to overcome? Are there areas of your life that you find a lack? Are there parts of yourself that you do not believe are worthy of, or able to be, loved? Face them. See that the fear is in your mind and not in the situation. Begin writing. Know that the ink on the page does not bind you. It is the fear that has been fused to the memory, the way in which it is remembered, the way in which it was not processed, that allows the pain to resonate. It is you that holds on. It is you that can let go. It is not your fault, dear one, that the pain was created. It is now your responsibility to make a choice. Will I face my reflection, or will I continue to avoid it? Will I see my boat as anchored, or will I see it a floating to its destination? Please write now. You are worth this time. You have always been worth this time. Please invest what you are able to give. Without awareness, there can be no action. Begin.

_____

_____

_____

_____

_____

_____

_____

_____

_____

_____

_____

_____

Love is the greatest of currencies. It is more valuable than gold or diamond. With it, I am able to purchase the intangible. It is the missing piece of my puzzle. In fact, it is the entire puzzle. It allows us to clearly see the picture. If we are comparing our love, the love is untrue. If we are saying, "My love is stronger," "My love is better," or "My love is purer," then we are speaking of pride, which is a lack of love. We are allowing the superego (the judge, jury, executioner, society, the box in which we have been placed) to speak. That is not love. Money will purchase things that will eventually fade, rust, tarnish, erode and lose value. Money will buy things that do not care for me. Money buys the house. Love buys the home.

I am my only obstacle. I am everything that I allow myself to believe. I am the anchor. I am the sail.

If you spoke the words, "I am enough," would you believe?

This meditation is going to discuss pain. I will ask that you visualize it and give it form. I use a black tornado or sometimes just a colorless mass. It depends on the questioning of the prompts. Do what you are able to do. You need never do any more than what is possible. Do not create a strain. If you uncovered trauma, seek professional care through a licensed therapist or mental health counselor. There is no shame in seeking help outside of you. We are meant to help others. We are meant to be helped by others.

Arrive at this moment. Allow yourself to find comfort here. Begin taking deep breaths. Lower your shoulders. Unclench your jaw. Take your tongue off the roof of your mouth. Feel the air enter your lungs. Feel the tips of your fingers. Feel your eyelids and your mouth. Do you notice any area of tension in your body? If anything is tightened, simply loosen it. Feel your lungs as they expanded, continuing to bring you life. Feel the areas beneath you. Know that it is a solid form and that it supports you at this moment. You are safe. You are protected in this sacred space. See yourself as if you are looking down upon your body.

Bring a form to a negative emotion that was listed. What is its color? Does it have an aroma? How much space does it take up? Are you able to see it? What is its texture? Is it solid? Does it move or is it fixed in position? See that it cannot harm you unless you allow harm to be brought to you. You no longer have to accept. This thing that you see now, know that it has no power over you unless you give power to it. Feel your power. Notice your heartbeat. With every beat feel your power grow. Feel your ability to make a choice. Feel your strength begin to rise inside of you. Know that this strength has been there all along. This strength, this power, will always be there. Feel it at this moment. See your object as weakening. Do you see that your object now trembles? You and this object desire the same thing… love. Invite your pain and fear to come and sit with you, knowing it cannot harm you. When you stop fighting and resisting its presence, it transforms into a gift. When you offer this object your love, it shows you your gift. You no longer have to run from discomfort. You no longer have to see vulnerability as a weakness or something to be avoided. You no longer have to see an obstacle as unmovable. Your thoughts will move mountains because your mountains are your thoughts.

See yourself seated in a darkened room. Remember that fear has no place in this room. You are the creator of this room. You chose what to include. Look down upon yourself as though you are seated in a balcony. You are the only thing you can see in this room. With every deepened breath watch as the light that comes from you begin to illuminate your surroundings. Feel your gift, your love, bring life to whatever exists in this space with you. Is it your home? Are you outside? Are you on that red-sand beach or cabin surrounded by beautiful, abundant mountains? The power of your love will bring radiance to all you come in contact with once it takes root in your heart. When we oppose the current moment, when we see life as anchored, we are stating right now isn't good enough. As without, so within. Our external perceptions mirror our internal definition. When I feel inadequate, when I feel scared, when I feel less than, all of my experiences with the world and reality will be lessened and diminished.

If I am to love myself, I must drop the mask and expose the wounds. I must bring love to all the wounded parts of myself. My wounds will only heal when love is applied. I stop betraying myself when love is applied. I will enter my power and I will remember my strength when love is applied.

When I sit in stillness, I remember that infinite wisdom lies within.

Imagine your world, being illuminated from the light within you. If you spoke the words, "I am enough," would you believe?

Without Awareness...

What can be done about a thing unknown? Am I able to change what I cannot see? Without awareness, there can be no action.

Are you able to identify areas in your life that you need to change? Are you willing to shine a light on areas that have previously gone unexposed? Are you willing to stir the waters of stagnation in order to move out of them? If you answered yes, then let's begin. Write out areas, that you are aware of, that need change or resolution in your life. Spend more than a few minutes on this. Please, do not skip ahead.

_____

_____

_____

_____

_____

_____

_____

_____

_____

_____

_____

_____

_____

_____

How did that feel? Look back over the list and identify what this list creates within you. Is it motivating? Is it frightening? Does it feel more real now that you got these thoughts out of your mind and onto paper? You get to decide what this list makes you feel.

The prompt was to write about areas that need changed, not write about areas you *want* to change. Desire is different in each one of us. Allow yourself to be exactly where you are. You needn't be anywhere but here, now. Return to this list and star the items that you are not yet ready to change. It's okay. No one will see this list. You will not be judged or condemned for not being ready. If you remember, you are the judge and jury. I am not in that courtroom. Neither is another. Please, do this now before moving forward. (It is in this action that you are, in fact, moving forward).

I will say this if you are waiting for motivation to strike you… it may not. The biggest motivator is momentum, which is only created by movement. You cannot wait on movement to strike you. You cannot wait for an action to be done to you. You are that action. You are that desire and drive. You are the determination. You have a choice on the role you will play in your story. Who else will create but the author?

Now ask yourself this question: What would it take for me to want to change the areas that are starred?

Remind yourself that lack is perception based.
Whatever you need, you already have. Every
capability to change/improve comes from within. It
does not come from me, but from you.

I recently asked if you were ready to shine the light
on areas previously unexposed. Let's put that to the
test. Let's see how ready you truly are. If you find
yourself *here*, in this sacred moment, then you are
ready. You have been ready. If you are really
moved to make a difference in your life, ask for
feedback. We have a window from which we view
the world. According to psychologists Joseph Luft
and Harrington Ingham, it looks like this:

Johari Window

	Known to self	Not known to self
Known to others		
	Arena	Blind Spot
Not Known to Others		
	Façade	Unknown

For the sake of space, the picture has been reduced.
However, the meaning has not. Asking for feedback

from people who know you best is like bringing light into the blind spot on our pane. If a blind man walks into a wall, is it his fault? If you are a witness, are you at fault? Or is "fault" a word we shouldn't even use in this scenario? How often do we assign fault to a scenario that is unnecessary?

If you are willing to ask for help, who will you ask? Will you only ask one person? Will you get feedback from multiple sources? Will you inquire about one area to a parent and in another area to a friend? Will you ask a single friend for advice on marriage? Will you ask a friend without children for advice on being a parent? Or will you be selective?

A key to remember: Loved ones can be our biggest support, but they can also be our biggest critic. Will you fly in "blind" when asking for feedback? (I do not recommend this tactic). Perhaps setting the tone will disallow room for misinterpretation or adopting the victim mentality. If you want to go through your obstacle, being a victim will not get you there. Misinterpreting will not either. Remind the person to use "I statements" and to speak from their personal experience. If something doesn't involve them, they should not speak on it. (IE. An uncle telling you how you offended your aunt, or a friend speaking on the behalf of another friend). No one will ever clearly get across the point of another. Be ready to hear things that may be difficult to hear. Remind yourself that this is what you want. Remind yourself that your greatest strength is often in simply standing when you want to run. Do not avoid the thorn any longer, remove it. Removing the thorn will involve pain, but it is less than the pain of avoiding the thorn. Choose to hear the words of feedback without judgment. "Bad" behavior does not constitute a "bad" person. Above all else, tell this person that you are practicing being vulnerable and exposed. Be honest. Acknowledge your work! If you need to cry, cry. But do not run. Listen. Feel. Make eye contact. Hold their hand. Thank them for their feedback. It is important to remember to ask for honesty. Ask them to remove emotions from the occurrence, if able, and provide the facts. If a moment becomes elevated, take a timeout, but return to complete this work. How many times has work begun in you without being completed? Will you allow this to continue to be your process? Or will you allow progress to take you? The way we learn how not to burn is by walking through the fire, not around it. Awareness is a necessity. It is your anchor, or it is your sail.

Be gentle but remove the blinders. It is time. There is only now. There is only ever now.

Imagine the gift of awareness encompassing you and guiding you forward. If you said aloud, "I am enough," would you believe?

Find yourself at this moment seated or resting comfortably.

Close your eyes and take 3 deep exhales, but do not allow them to be without noise. Push out the stale energy, force out the things from the past that you want to release. Feel the old tapes leaving on your breath.

Take one more deep breath, but on this exhale, feel relief. Let it be likened to the first calmed breath after a marathon or the first caught breath after a sacred vow. Slow it down. Slacken your shoulders. Take your tongue off the roof of your mouth. Just be for a few moments. Exist, fully alive, in this space. You are worth the time.

Bring to mind the word "peace." Repeat this word. Allow it to resonate and echo as if you were in a large auditorium without other noise. You are the only one here. And you are not, at this moment, fearful of being alone. Your only desired outcome of this moment is peace. Continue repeating this word. Slow your internal speech. Deepen your breathing. Notice any areas of discomfort in your body and relax that area.

What would it take for you to experience peace in your life? What would it take for you to experience peace in all of your moments? What are you able to do, right now, in order to experience peace despite all obstacles? Must you change your mind or outlook? Are you waiting on some external force to change in order for you to experience peace? Does someone else or something else have control over the way you feel? Do you not remember that you are the movement? Have you forgotten that you are the author and creator of your story? Are you able to recall that the way in which you view the world creates your reality? Are you creating a reality of peace? Are you creating a reality of chaos? What you call out to, calls back to you. If you call out, in this sacred space, peace, then the echo will be peace. If you call out anger, the response will be anger. Your echo begins with your thoughts. All things begin with your thoughts. Are you willing to practice synchronizing your heart with your mind? What if all things began with our hearts? How greater would the outcome be? What areas of your life would improve, or change, if you felt with your heart, instead of thought with your mind? What else will you feel at this moment?

I will ask you now to bring the word "love" to your attention. See the word. Feel the word. What does love mean to you? I do not speak of conditioned love, nor rewarded love, nor deserving love. I refer to complete and total acceptance without attempting to change any aspect or detail of another. I refer to forgiving love. I refer to undying love. I refer to love that grows because of the fire, not smolders.

Find yourself again in this auditorium, without fear. What is preventing you from feeling love? In what ways are you the barrier? What are you able to do, at this moment, to dissolve your barrier? If love does not come from within, how then, can it come from without? If you love yourself based upon condition, then you will love all others based upon condition. If you find moments in which love flows and moments in which love stands stagnant, what is in the way? Picture a flowing river being blocked. The trees, plants and all life on the other side of this block are withering from the lack of water. Do you see that you are the life that withers? Do you see that you are that block? It is not another. It is not the past. It is not some future anxiety preventing today from being created fully alive. Whatever capability you need to feel peace and to feel loved, you already have. You must no longer wait on the dam to be cleared. You must remember that you are the force that clears it.

If I am to increase my awareness, then I must ask questions that I have been afraid to ask. Return to the auditorium. Decorate it. Allow this place to feel welcoming and inviting. Let warm, radiating light enter this place. You are the author. You are the constructor. You are no less Divine than the wind that moves the trees. How much greater can your purpose be?

Imagine the gift of awareness encompassing you and guiding you forward. If you said aloud, "I am enough," would you believe?

Vulnerable Creativity

"What's the greater risk? Letting go of what people think – or letting go of how I feel, what I believe, and who I am?"

-Brené Brown

Everything involving creativity takes a risk. The greater the investment, the greater the return. If the risk you are willing to take is behind closed doors, how will you ever get feedback? How will you move forward? How many times have you practiced or rehearsed a speech, conversation, piece of music, etc. only to have it go every way but the way you rehearsed? Probably most of the time. Practice, learn, increase fluidity, but take it to an arena in which you can receive input and construction. You may be able to build a house by yourself, but an extra set of hands and an extra set of eyes will allow things to be seen that would otherwise remain hidden.

I had a conversation with a young man that had spent many years of his life attempting to be seen in a way that did not resonate with his internal being. He told me, through tears, that he would spend hundreds of dollars on name brand shoes, pants and t-shirts in order to be seen in a certain way by people who were younger than him. He commented that he "wanted people to be like him." However, he identified that he does not know who he is. How can someone be like him if his "identity" is wrapped up in items? This young man was turning himself in on a warrant that he had been, in his words, "running from for a long time." I asked him what else he is running from. He divulged, "I got all these tattoos and I talk a certain way because I didn't want people to hurt me. I threaten to hurt people over little things. I'm really a teddy bear. I care so much about people, but I spend every possible moment building my ego." He said he is understanding that "it doesn't matter what other people think anymore." He would go on to tell me about people who he "led down the wrong path." All of his emotional outpouring and self-discoveries were telling him who he really is. Will he listen and truly make this change? Will he allow himself to remain vulnerable in order to create his true identity? I really hope so. I believe in him, but does he believe in himself? I guess we will see.

In order for me to create an identity, it is necessary for me to uncover what it is I don't like. Failure will teach you what you don't like and what you don't want to tolerate. It can keep you in place, or it can propel you. Those are the two options. All of the great leaders you read about, all the gurus and guides, the prophets and the preachers, they look in the mirror and see themselves as fallible and human. Their identities are made up of attempts and failures, scars and beauty. All of our identities are, but are you willing to see? Are you willing to be vulnerable in order to determine who you are? Are you willing to submit your resume when you know there may be a better candidate? Are you willing to stand up and give that presentation when you are certainly not the most knowledgeable on that subject? Are you willing to be brave in the face of personal fear? Are you willing to love unconditionally even though it may mean heartbreak? Are you willing to let go of what someone thinks of you in order to discover a passion? The greater the investment, the greater the return. You are worth the investment.

I remember having felt this young man's pains. I would bottle up my difficult emotions, they would finally spill out, I would climb out from behind my wall, let my pain be seen by someone close to me, cry and share my feelings, stop crying, feel better, and then think "it's not that bad, I was just having a moment. I'm fine now." The truth is, when someone says, "I'm fine," it means leave me alone. Fine is not fine. And it's okay to be not fine. But we live in a society that has taught us to suck it up, walk it off, everyone is depressed, if you're truly depressed take this pill, you don't need to work through your baggage, and be a man. This is not the message I received from my family, but perhaps you did. Maybe you were taught the societal myths about manhood, or womanhood. Maybe you were taught that your worth is determined upon your stuff or your output. I know a lot of miserable rich people. And I know a lot of unhappy doctors.

I had a woman recently tell me it is "normal" for her to be "anxious." There were no triggers or anxiety cues present. She's just "an anxious person" per her report. At one point in time, this was not the case. But today it is. When I attempt to go into this anxiety, she becomes visibly uncomfortable and asks to not talk about it. There are reasons. But she is not willing to risk being seen in all her scars and beauty. She tells herself she is not worth this investment. She doesn't see that her worth is mountainous. But how can you see the mountains behind a wall? How would you know they even existed? When someone speaks of them, you disbelieve because you cannot see them for yourself. And then you become angry and think they are lying or telling you what they want you to hear. You cannot understand their truth if you are unwilling to step out and seek.

How willing are you to step out and create? What is it that you are really risking? Are you perhaps making something harder than it needs to be? Do you have the burden of overthinking? Or you magnifying or possibly minimizing this risk? Are you comparing a previous experience to all future ones? Do you expect the same result or failure to occur again and again and it prevents you from trying? If there is no threat to physical harm or loss of life or limb, then what good excuse do you have to prevent you from growth and expansion?

What is it that you are desiring to achieve from this risk? Is it something tangible, like a promotion, romantic partnership, or some type of noun that can be touched? Or is it something intangible like a deeper connection to God or some emotion that moves you? What is it that you are attempting to cultivate and manifest? Call it out. Write it down. Begin to see your life as already having achieved your outcome. If it is a thing, how will it improve you? If it is an emotion, how will you use it to help others?

Finally, what is your level of confidence that this goal can be achieved, but also that this goal can be achieved by you? Robert Kiyosaki said, "If you want to change your life, begin by changing your words. Start speaking the words of your dreams, of who you want to become, not the words of fear or failure." If you look for reasons you will fail, you will find them everywhere. They will become all that you see. You will interpret and misinterpret every stone on your path. If you look for reasons you will succeed, you will find them everywhere. You will hear a person's truth, even if you cannot see it for yourself, you will believe them and allow them to guide you. You will walk beside them, in your scars and your beauty, and you will know that you are worth the investment. Their truth will become a shared view; one you can hold instead of dismissing.

Are you willing to be seen, in all your fallible glory? Are you willing to look in a mirror or stand in front of an audience and say, "Here I am in all my pride and fear" or will you continue to determine your worth to be less than the wind and without purpose? How much greater is your worth than what creates the tides and moves the leaves?

If you were to stand in the auditorium, decorated with your touch, warmed from the sunlight and filled with faces of those you love, would you be able to state, "I am enough" and believe?

This next portion includes an activity that is not a guided meditation, however, I will detail a way in which you could use this information and exercise to lead you into a guided meditation.

I am going to create a list identifying various character strengths and I want you to identify your top ten most important strengths. I am not asking you to detail the ten you are best at. I am asking to circle, star, mark, underline, etc. the ten that resonates most with you.

Adaptability

Appreciation

Bravery

Compassion

Connection/Purpose

Creativity

Curiosity

Dependability

Enthusiasm

Fairness

Forgiveness

Gratitude

Hope/Optimism

Humility

Humor

Integrity

Kindness

Leadership

Love

Learning

Open-mindedness

Perspective

Perseverance

Respectfulness

Self-control

Social Intelligence

Spirituality

Teamwork

_____

_____

_____

_____

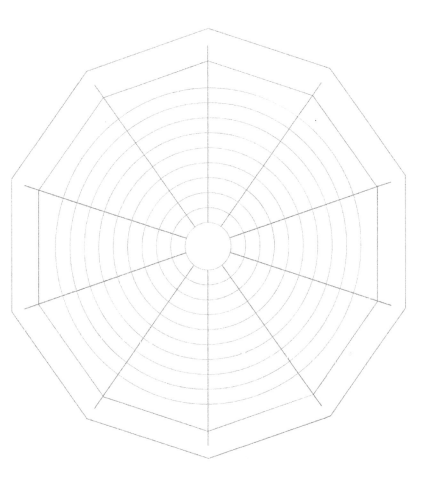

After you have made your selection, go back and rate them on a scale of 1-10. 1 meaning highly dissatisfied and 10 being fully satisfied. Then insert them into the graph below. The next page will show what a completed graph will look like.

Inputting your information into this graph is a
symbolic way of viewing the balance, or most
likely, imbalance you are experiencing. If you want
to change, you can. If you really want to practice
vulnerability, ask someone who knows you best to
rate you on your list.

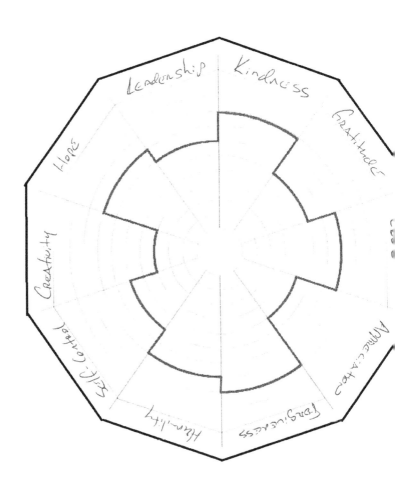

Take an honest assessment of your graph. Is this where you are, or is this where you want to be? Would someone who knows you best rate you differently? Perhaps the person who knows you best would rate you based on a negative emotion or hidden resentment. Perhaps the relationship has gone stale or there is anger involved. I encourage you to practice vulnerability by asking someone who knows the real you but also supports and encourages you. Ask someone who has no veiled agenda against you for their feedback.

If there is an area that you wish you raise the number, do not attempt to jump from a 3 to an 8. Allow the 3 to become a 4. That is good enough. Acknowledge the progress. It is unrealistic to move multiple numbers in a day or a few moments. You cannot simply meditate one time and all your problems become solutions. You must create a practice that you will adhere to in order to become who you know you are able to be.

I completed this exercise myself. As I have already said, I do everything I ask another to do. I determined my scores to be all 7s, 8s, and 9s. I completed my graph and felt pretty good about my answers. I believe God stepped in with the question, "Is there where I am or where I want to be?" And then the twist was added, "Would someone who knows me best rate me differently?" I know that when I am hungry, or tired, or maybe I've had a long day at work, or maybe I'm not feeling cared about (based most likely upon false interpretations) I will not display all 7s, 8s, and 9s. I live in a world where I am able to purchase food. I am not saying that food is a meaningless thing, what I am saying is that a thing like hunger, which I am able to get around, can create such a dissonance within me and stand in the way of what is most important to me, and I will act accordingly. And sleep. I operate the same off of 5 hours that I do 9, but somewhere in my mind when I'm tired, I don't come off as forgiving or loving or grateful. How can something so relatively small make such a profound impact on my life that I am able to be seen in a light in which I would not tolerate in another? Am I making sense? If I let something small stand in the way of being connected with God, people and myself, what will I do when something actually important interferes? Will I run? Will I cower? Will I freeze? Will I say, "I didn't sleep well last night," or "I didn't get to eat lunch today so I can't respond appropriately?"

Let's all hope not.

To repeat, the best motivation is momentum. Momentum is gained by continuing. Motivation is increased by doing. Awareness is increased by asking. And creativity comes through vulnerability.

The following guided meditation is a body scan meditation. When you scan the different parts of the body, you are creating space for tense areas to relax.

This meditation can assist you with falling asleep when troubled or in becoming grounded when emotionally elevated.

I will first ask you to take a few moments to settle into a comfortable position. Find yourself being relaxed while also being alert. Stand, sit, lay down, whichever position feels most appropriate for you. There is no "wrong way" to meditate.

When starting your scan, begin at your toes. Notice any areas of discomfort as you move up your body. You can tense or tighten them if you choose. Slowly make your way up to your ankles and into your lower legs. Feel your knees and your thighs. There is no need to rush through this process. Take your time. Enjoy this sacred moment. Pay attention to your hips, pelvis and tail bone. Are you able to feel your stomach? Do you notice any tension in your stomach? Perhaps is it where you hold anxiety. Find yourself relaxing in each area you pass. Slowly make your way up through your torso. Pass through your ribcage, chest, and spine. Continue deep breathing and feel the expanse of your lungs as you breathe. See your lungs filling with air and the air passing through your veins into your bloodstream. Are you able to feel your heartbeat? Know that every beat of your heart is sending love and energy throughout your system. Work up to your shoulders. Do you notice any tension in this area? What about your posture? Are you slouched? Have you straightened your spine into alignment? Move down now through your arms, into your elbows, your wrists, and your hands. Come back up through your arms into your neck. Feel your face. Bring awareness to your ear lobes, your brow and the tip of your nose. Is your jaw tightened? Is your tongue on the roof of your mouth? Slackened your facial muscles. Go up to the top of your head and notice your crown. Hold your body into complete and total awareness for one last observation.

Notice what you feel as you scan through your body without judgment. Heighten consciousness on all physical sensations, on your skin, muscle, and bone. Note areas of tension and those that feel slightly more opened or relaxed.

All things simply are. There is no wrong or should not be. There is no good. There is no bad. You are merely noticing what you notice. You will have areas that are more difficult to tap into than others. You may find one side feels different than the other.

Notice any difference, great or small, from the first moment of this meditation to the current moment.

Now that we are grounded, bring an area of character that you listed in the exercise in this chapter. What would it feel like for that area to be whole? What it is that you need in order to move that number higher? Bring this area into closer focus. Feel it. Allow this strength to encompass and surround you. Do you know that you have all you need to bring this area to a heightened state? Ask yourself, "What can I do to bring my heightened state to others?" "What can I do to bring awareness to the areas of my life that I want to change?" "Who am I willing to be vulnerable around as a way to increase what is most important to me?"

If you spoke the words, "I am enough," from your heightened state, would you believe?

The Way Out of Shame

Forgiving yourself is the door opening that, when walked through, will allow you to become the greatest version of yourself. If you had the opportunity to go back in time and re-do or un-do your experiences, would you? In going back and undoing, you are also un-learning all of the lessons involving these experiences. Would going back really be worth it? If we went back and re-lived our lives, would we not participate in the same actions? After all, we are still the same person who chose to participate in our experiences we wish to un-do. What we do not learn, we repeat.

Guilt may be what other people say about you, but shame is what you are saying about you. Shame is a secret that we keep closely hidden. It is most likely seen by everyone in the way we carry ourselves, and it runs our life. It hinders our interactions and gets in the way of things we wish we could do but tell ourselves we can't. Shame is the feeling that goes unspoken even though we wear it so loudly. Shame is what we don't want others to see. Shame is the story you tell yourself at night when you can't sleep. Shame is the reason you believe yourself to be inadequate or "not good enough." Shame is only healed when you call it by name. What you call by name is no longer a secret. You work *through* shame by bringing it out of the darkness and into the light. What grows in the dark, dies in the light.

Guilt is based upon a previous action. Shame is based upon replaying that action over and over and tying a specific meaning to that action.

We tell ourselves, I did this behavior, this behavior is bad, therefore I am bad. We don't see that this is what we are doing, but we are doing it. And when "I am bad" I may continue with a behavior that I no longer want to do because I now believe myself to be unredeemable. Shame is not based upon a failure; it is the constant reminding yourself that you *are* that failure. You become one with that failure, you are fused, and you are synced with failure. The story we then tell ourselves is that "I am a mistake."

Guilt is "I made a mistake." Shame is "I am a mistake." And nothing could be more untrue.

When we experience shame, we can also get caught up in blaming. Instead of bringing my shame into the light, I bring someone else's, or I project my shame onto whoever is closest to me. It's much easier to look at another's reflection than it is to look at our own. When we begin telling ourselves a story that something is the fault of another, we are refusing to accept our role and we find ourselves stuck. And we remain stuck until we acknowledge our role. Shame is a secondary emotion, similar to anger. I would say anger is not a true emotion. It's the mask that hides the true emotion- pain. We are taught, or shown by the demonstration of others, that anger is appropriate and "normal," and that addressing pain is not. I spoke with a young man today who referred to his family's "tradition of not addressing what is uncomfortable." His role model, his father, a military man, successful, self-made and very respected, taught him avoidance. Perhaps it was a subliminal message, however, through tears, he told me he doesn't live up to the expectation that was set for him, by his father. He said, "I was supposed to be in the military." I inquired, "Why did you want to be in the military?" He responded, "Because it's what my father did." This young man becomes somewhat defensive when I stated his desire to be in the service was not his own, but that of his father. He felt he has "let him down." In truth, he let himself down because he never developed his own identity. He currently does not know what he wants to do as a career. However, he was able to identify "I want to help people."

This young man typically fills the rooms with words. It is his shame, his unhealthy perception of self, that has prevented him from progressing. But how can you progress into what you do now know you want to be? This was the first real conversation this person had with me. After months of talking, he finally spoke. He acknowledged his discomfort and it became bearable. Interesting how this process works. When I face what I want to avoid, I progress. We can spend years attempting to control, avoid or deflect our discomforts. And in moments, we can begin our healing process. Have you been avoiding healing? If so, how much longer do you need? Can you begin today? (The answer is yes). But will you?

When I ask people what they see as their worst flaws or inadequacies, things they do not often disclose, they identify things such as "impulsivity, dishonesty, distrust, quick to make assumptions, procrastination/hesitation, short-fused, intolerant, lessened self-worth and confidence, quick to feel judged, quick to judge others, negative self-talk, past history of abuse/trauma, past history of abusing another, substance abuse, self-harm, perfectionism" and so on and so on. When I ask, "If a friend disclosed this information to you, how would you respond?" The answers are always some form of compassion, sympathy, empathy, acceptance, understanding, and love. When I ask how they tend to be towards themselves with these same thoughts and feelings, the answer is the opposite. We show empathy to another person who is experiencing lessened self-worth, yet we do not tolerate it in ourselves nor do we provide ourselves with the same grace and mercy we so fluently give to others.

What do you see as your inadequacies?

How do you treat yourself regarding what you listed?

When do you feel most defeated?

What situations from your past do you feel the most shame around?

When a friend is having a hard time, how do you tend to be toward that person?

If you are having a hard time, how do you tend to be toward yourself?

What is the obstacle to becoming a friend to yourself?

What do you fear might happen if you were to be kinder and more compassionate with yourself?

List persons by name that you are willing to discuss what you have kept hidden. List the time and day in which you will begin this discussion.

Commit.

∞

The scared child within each one of us needs to heal. But in order to heal, we have to first acknowledge. When you first read the words "scared child," what did you feel?

To be honest, I have struggled with this part of the book. I didn't know how to write it, or at least, that was the story I was allowing myself to believe. I flirted with my distractions, I got "busy" with life and I made the excuses. I knew I wanted to write a meditation based upon the scared child, however, I didn't know where to begin. I got caught up worrying about exactly what to write. I was paying attention to the words and not their meaning. I was concentrating on writing a meditation, in order to follow suit with the way the other chapters have ended... However, each chapter is its own. One is not the other, nor does it need to be. (Even twins have their own preferences). In allowing this chapter to be its own subject, I will ask that we do things with a slight variance. I want us to write a letter to the scared child that lives within. The only parameters or instructions are these: Write a letter to the scared child within. Tell this child (which is you) all the things you did not hear or did not feel that will allow healing to take place. Do not do what I did with this chapter. Do not allow a month to pass without progress. You are the child. You know better than anyone else what to say. Your voice is what is most important to this child. It has been speaking to your inner child throughout the entirety of your life. You may need to change the script or just simply pay attention to the words and their meanings. As always, I will never ask you to do something I have not done. I am also writing a letter. And it is included below.

Dearest one,

I am here to give you love. It is the only thing I am here to offer. It is the only subject I wish to speak.

I hear you. I see you. I feel you. You are Divinely created. You have a purpose that only you can fulfill. The day you were born was the day you were destined to enter this world. You are here to make an impact and you are just the way you for many reasons. I do not know them all. But these reasons will find you, in their own time. You have many

*questions. And I encourage you to ask them. I
encourage you to explore and find out what you like
and what you enjoy. I want you to learn through
failings and creativity. It is okay to fail. It is okay to
not be any other but yourself. You have a specific
skill set that is not like any other person or being.*

*Little one, you will struggle. And in that struggle,
you will learn your ability to walk and create, to
stand and fall, to stumble and soar. You will find
greatness within you through moments of self-doubt
and distrust. You will uncover strength through
moments of pain. You will find rivers of peace and
serenity by going through valleys of pain and
weakness. The greatness within you will call out to
the greatness within another. People will want to be
like you, but only when you learn to accept yourself
exactly as you are.*

*There is nothing wrong with you, dearest one. You
are only limited by what you allow yourself to
become limited by. You can do anything. Whatever
you desire, you are able to become. Whatever title
you wish you hold, go after it. Whatever thing you
wish to achieve, you will do it. Just know that things
do not define you. Your heart is the most precious
thing you have been given. "Out of the abundance
of the heart, the mouth speaks." Be careful what
you let into your heart. Do not give your heart away
but allow it to be felt by all who come in contact
with you.*

Always speak with kindness, to others and to yourself.

You are worth everything, little one. Do not ever forget how Divine you are. The One who created the infinite space used the same thoughts to create you. How much more important are you than empty, infinite space?

_ _

At the moment, my son is 3 months old. I was feeding him around midnight last night (this morning), and I recalled my need to write my letter to the scared child. I have done this previously in past group exercises, but I didn't want to just do it to check a box. I wanted to do it justice. I pictured myself at that age being held, but it was by my mother. My father never held me. He didn't enter my life until decades later. It was at that moment, early this morning, that a cycle was broken. I spoke these words to him aloud. Not exactly as they are typed, but the feelings and emotions are the same. The struggles that I experienced allowed for healing to take place in another- my son. He will always know the depth of his father's love. He will never have to question what I think about him or what I feel about him. His scared child will not be the sum of my equation. I will not contribute to his lessened self-worth. He will never question my intent or presence. He will not ask God open-ended questions about why I wasn't around, or if I love him; or if I even wanted him. He will know.

And he only knows because of my suffering. All suffering has a purpose. I did not find that purpose until many, many years later. I would go through it again in order to break this cycle. But in the moment of pain, we just wish it away.

Speak about your shame. What grows in the dark, dies in the light.

Sit in comfort and begin breathing deeply. Pay attention to any discomfort and release tension in that area. Reflect upon your letter after its completion. *Please, do not move forward until this has been completed.* Feel the effect of the emotions shared bringing relief to internally pained areas of your scared child. Sit in these sacred moments for as long as you will. Return to them often.

Embrace your scared child.

Once love flows from within, it can begin to flow without. The second will not work without the first.

If you spoke the words, "You are enough," to your scared child, would they believe?

What Have You Forgotten?

"Be who you are and say what you feel, because those who mind don't matter, and those who matter don't mind."

-Dr. Seuss

It is interesting that we were just speaking of the scared child, and the quote that sticks out to me, as we enter this next chapter, is a man who wrote for children.

I am going to ask you to think back to an age where other people's opinions didn't matter. As you reflect on that period of time, begin to see how life was different. Was life any better? Was life any worse? Refrain from getting in your head about this answer. Enter your heart (hopefully, you are already there). Ask your heart about how life was different. You will notice fewer complex answers when you enter your heart. Things simply are. But perhaps you are not there yet. This is not a right or a wrong. Just be where you are.

When I ask people when they began being concerned or aware of other's viewpoints, the average age I hear in response is between 7 or 8 years old. As an adult (being in my head about the answer), I can explain away my child-like wonder and mislabel it for lack of awareness of what the "real world" is like. When I think back of the way in which I viewed beauty in the world, the adult wants to tell me of the hidden ugliness, and the "people out to gct you." When I think of being a child and only having in the moment (mindfulness) type thinking, the adult (thinking mind) will tell me, "That's because you didn't have a mortgage and food to pay the bill for. You didn't have any concerns about growing up or aging. You weren't aware of all the pain that is to come in life." And that is the way that our minds speak to our hearts.

As we continue this work on ourselves, our vision begins to expand. You cannot climb a higher mountain with the same vision in which you sat in a valley. You cannot write the follow-up to your best-selling novel with the same vision you had for the first. You must expand. To quote Les Brown and Les Brown's mentor, "You gotta be hungry!"

There was a study that stated 85% of self-talk is negative. I was researching this to make sure it was, in fact, correct when I came across an article that quoted that percentage to be 90%. To take this to a heightened sense of awareness, I will add another quote. Deepak Chopra stated, "We have approximately 60,000 thoughts in a day. Unfortunately, 95% of them are thoughts we had the day before." 95% of 60,000 is 57,000. There is no accurate calculation nor study, that I have found, to indicate how many of our thoughts are self-talk. There is one that suggests 80% of our thoughts are negative but it does not indicate to who or whom the negativity is directed.

What I get from these numbers is this: with the number of thoughts and re-occurring thoughts we have every day, how many of them are spoked to tear down either ourselves or another person? If I have these many thoughts flying around in my mind, every single day, am I paying attention to what are they telling me to believe? Or have they been there so long that I've already adopted what they have to say and made it my own? Do I already believe the message without paying attention to what it is saying?

Your mind will tell you that you are tired when you are not tired. It will tell you to stay seated when you want to stand. It will tell you that no one wants to hear what you have to say. It will remind you of what you cannot do while it tells you why you cannot do it. Your mind will judge yourself while judging another. Your mind will remind you of the education you do not have and the experience you have not gained. It will remind you of where you came from and tell you that your story is not worth speaking. Your mind will fill you with fear. And in those moments, you must stand up and say, "I am afraid, but I am more afraid not to."

Now let us ask the question what have I forgotten? Which voice have I been listening to? If you are not listening to a voice that is your own, change the tape. If the tape is positive and encouraging, then tape over it in your own voice. Do not allow another to speak for you any longer. Bring to mind people you are closest to and most comfortable with. How do you act around them? What is your manner of thinking like when you are around people who know the real you? Is there a difference in actions around people you don't know as well? Why? If you are able to identify a difference in actions when you in these two separate groups, are you hindered? Does fear of rejection prevent you from being your real self? Does a need to be liked and accepted keep you within a box? What is it that prevents you from being unboxed or uncaged?

Is there a hardship in life where a lesson was taught but you have forgotten? In working with addicts for many years and being in recovery for 11 years (so far) myself, I often see and hear people speak of forgetting their pain. When we forget our pain, we return to what harms us. Think of how this statement is true in your life. Without awareness, there can be no action. Have you returned to a painful place or somewhere you left but have found yourself back, stuck, in an environment you wish to no longer be in? What is the voice telling you as you are in this place? What will it take to bring you out of pain? I believe the steps in this book will assist and already have assisted. Keep speaking. Pay attention. Continue and commit.

Back to the title of this chapter...

(I do not want to write this next part, but I must).

My grandmother "mamaw" has been a staple in my life. My grandfather died when I was 13 and my father has never been around. I was raised mostly by women. I have an uncle, who is wonderfully kind and gentle. However, growing up, he was very intimidating. He is assertive. Which to me just looked like a very dominant trait, of which I had no dominant traits. He was kind. But I was intimidated by him, so I did not often seek him out for guidance. Hence, raised mostly by women. My brother and I were at mamaw's house after school, overnight, went to church with her, etc. She has always been very, very involved in my life. After papaw's death, we moved in with my mamaw to a different house. It was the house my mom and her siblings were raised in. She let me live with her no matter what. When I dropped out of college and came back home, I just went back to living with mamaw. Throughout the many years of substance abuse I participated in, she still let me live there. She accepted me no matter what. She did not condone my behaviors in any way, but she never kicked me out. The last and final time I "called out for help," we found a place, but it was a 50-60 minute drive, one-way and I had to get there every day to get my "medicine." I did not have a car at this time, nor did I have any real income. My mamaw drove me most days and paid the $13 a day it cost to medicate me, so I didn't experience withdrawal. This went on for 9 months until I completed the program. Every day. 9 months. She paid for me to get well again. Even after taking so much from her. She never gave up on me. She always says, "Babe, look how far we've come!" She has no idea of her impact on me. Words wouldn't even begin to speak it.

Why am I telling you this?

Mamaw was diagnosed with dementia around 2 years ago, I believe. It was early-onset, so she was able to live in her home, the home I mentioned earlier, for a while, but it just became too much for her to take care of on her own. When the time came, she was transitioned to an assisted living facility. I would take my daughter to visit her on my off days and we would go out to eat. As her memory began getting worse, I began not going as often. I couldn't carry a one-year-old and help mamaw walk at the same time by myself. Or at least, that was my excuse. I noticed I began distancing myself from the person who means more to me than anything. The person who has impacted me in such a way that I quote her often in my therapy sessions to clients. The person who literally paid for me to stay "well" enough to get back on my feet and continue living. The person who taught me "My clothes are not what matters most, nor how handsome I may be. What matters is what I am inside, where only God can see." She is one of the few people who helped teach me to believe in myself and to stand up for others. And I started avoiding seeing her because of pain. I was unaware of this at first. I began asking myself questions, some of the ones I have written in this book, to search for reasoning. Subconsciously I began to believe when she passes, it won't hurt as bad. In a cowardly attempt to avoid pain, I put distance in between me and my mamaw. As I write in this sacred moment, she is still living. So, there is still time. Don't every let pain keep you from experiencing joy and love, or from making memories.

Will it take a loss for you to remember you love someone?

What is it we have forgotten? Have we forgotten what we love? Have we forgotten what we stand for or against? Have we forgotten how to laugh or have fun? Have we forgotten to experience life in all of its capacities? Have we forgotten to be grateful? Have we forgotten to be childlike and inquisitive? Have we forgotten how to give or to act without being reciprocated?

Have you forgotten how to forgive? Have you forgotten how to trust or empathize? Have you forgotten how to be creative or tolerant? Have you forgotten how to love? Have you forgotten how to feel belonging or joy? Have you forgotten your own freedom?

Have we forgotten how to have healthy expectations? Have we forgotten how to ask questions? Have we forgotten how to ask for feedback or what we want? Have we forgotten we were Divinely created?

Have you forgotten to say please? Have you forgotten to say thank you? Have you forgotten to remind yourself that everything is okay? Have you forgotten your own perfect beauty?

Have you forgotten that you are enough?

Go back and re-read these questions. Slowly. Absorb the content. Then respond. Through word or action.

Your meditation will be to focus on individual areas of response. Envision ways to increase and expand your current vision relating to these areas. Listen to soft music or sit in nature. Wherever you are, exist fully in that place. It is not the place that is important. It is you. It has always been you.

End the meditation on the words, "I am enough." From now on, end all your meditations on these words. It is not the words that are important. It is the message. You are the message.

The Only Way is Through

"The quickest way to where you are going is
through the fire, not around it."

-Me

How much of your time has been spent talking
yourself out of a goal you wish to achieve, or
something you desire to accomplish? If you can at
least identify one instance of this happening, then
you have allowed fear to speak louder than your
own voice. When you notice this dialogue
occurring, ask yourself: Do I believe in the obstacle,
or do I believe in the goal? Believing in the goal is
actually a belief in yourself and your own ability to
achieve that goal. It is not the goal that is of
importance; it is you. It is not the goal that
determines who we are or what we are capable of
completing. It is the process. It is the journey. It is
the dedication and strain that determines, to us and
the world, who we are. Most of us have spoken
words, often repeatedly, about things we are *going*
to do. Bring it to the present tense. Speak only of
what you are doing. Cut out the future tense. I am
not saying do not plan. Bring the focus here. Bring
the focus to the current step you are taking and exist
there fully. Anything worth doing is worth doing
badly. So, what if you fail? Make failure okay.
Make failure permittable. Make failure a lesson. It
is not the obstacle or the failure that stings; it is the
meaning we have applied.

I was speaking with a client one evening about not being employed in the career he desired due to drinking on the job. He reported anytime someone asks him about his job shame occurs followed quickly by anger, and fear. I asked what follows the fear, and he replied, "self-hatred." He went on to identify feeling "exposed, embarrassed, lonely and small." The way around for this man was to make a joke, respond with humor (deflection) and change the subject. This is not through. This is around. When we go around the obstacle, we are constantly going in circles, like water to a drain. Eventually, the obstacle will overpower us due to our walking endlessly around instead of through. This man had tied his identity to something he was no longer doing. He was lost, or at least, that is what he believed himself to be. He had applied the meaning that he is a failure due to a past situation, which he had very little control over. When he spoke of these moments, his posturing lowered, as did his tone of voice, almost to a whisper, as he sunk himself into the couch on which he saw sitting. He started speaking to the group members as if he was in front of judgmental co-workers at his former employer. I reminded him he is not on trial and highlighted his physical appearance. He again identified shame.

As previously stated, shame is a secret. When you expose it, it is no longer a shame. It begins to transform. I pointed out that by him being vulnerable to the group, he was beginning his journey of healing as to this specific regard. He pushed himself back up into a straightened posture after a simple acknowledgment of growth. It was a growth that he was unable to see but one that was visible to others in the room. I can see your face, but not my own.

I encouraged this man to begin identifying gratitude for his present moment. I gave him flashcards to write them down while he is at work. There was no excuse for this not to happen. When the mind shifts, the world shifts.

We go upstairs (to the mind) and look down on our problems, our obstacles, other people, expectations (met or unmet), etc. In order to go through the issue, we must come downstairs (to the heart). This is where our foundation is laid. The heart is where we begin the transformation. It is in the mind that our projections begin. It is in the mind where all denial originates. All of our defense mechanisms exist upstairs, away from our hearts. We must come downstairs to ground. Our views are obscured from upstairs. We must come downstairs to see properly what truly exists in front of us.

Our mind gives us excuses to avoid our obstacles. We begin using judgments and (mis)interpretations as reasoning to continue avoiding our progress. I do not believe we are aware we are doing this at the moment, but when we step back, we increase awareness. There is no justifiable reason to stay stuck. I have yet to hear a "good reason" to not work through an issue. Some obstacles may need a qualified therapist or a team of support persons, but all fear has a meaning. And the new meaning we must tie to the fear is to <u>move</u> <u>through</u>. How much longer are you going to allow yourself to remain stuck, unhinged, caged or controlled? When you are imprisoned, the only way out is through. When they are stuck in the mud, the only way out is through.

I recently asked groups of people, "What is something you want to let go?" Bellow, you will find varied responses:

"The past and worries about the future."

"Worthlessness and shame I feel for myself."

"Resentments towards my ex."

"Drugs and using."

"Negativity, past, judging others, thinking and worrying about the future."

"Fear that I will relapse and let everyone down."

"Anger and fear of my dad drinking himself to death."

"The disgust I have with my son's father."

"Worrying about what other people think, or what might happen, or about resentments, or about things that I can't do anything about."

"My anti-self-love complex."

"Feeling worthless, ugly, not good enough, broken, used, destroyed, and unlovable."

"Grief, shame, embarrassment, humiliation, worthless."

"How stagnant I have been."

"Anxiety, insecurity, and dependence (to feel safe)."

"Fear I might fall apart again and relapse."

"My obsessive thinking, impatience, irritability, restlessness and discontentment, worrying about what other people think."

"Feeling that I'm not good enough."

"Feeling of what life would have been like if I had children."

"An uneasiness with work colleagues about my situation, being afraid to go to a baseball game because it might trigger me to drink."

"Being afraid to talk in front of people because I don't have anything good to say."

"Not being intelligent enough."

"I want to let go of my fear in all aspects of my life. My life is ruled by fear of what people think of me… which leads me to be a compulsive people-pleaser because I want people to like me. And I want to let go of my resentments towards my mother and try to have more compassion for her. I think a lot of my people-pleasing comes from that relationship because all I ever wanted to do was make her happy."

The people above all have a longing to be loved and accepted. I will never feel accepted until I accept myself. All my beauty and all my scars. My mind will remind me of why I believe I am not good enough. Your voice is the most important thing you have. With it, you will speak life, or you will speak death. Pay attention to what you say.

On the other side of the paper, which they were unaware of, was another question, "Why haven't I let this go?" Below you will find some responses:

"I think I need to get therapy with a trauma therapist, but I haven't yet. I don't think I have the tools to change my perspective."

"I feel addicted to revisiting the past and thinking about the future. For some reason, my mind is far more interested in what is going on outside of my scope or life than it is on what's happening in front of me."

"I don't know how yet."

"I still think it was my fault for allowing myself to be put in that situation." (taking the blame that isn't yours)

"I will never understand her mentality and I think I need to figure it out and make sense of it all." (spending time on something they determine they "will never understand.")

"Dwelling on the past is a comfortable place." (comfort in the discomfort)

"I find some type of enjoyment holding onto my character defects. It makes me feel better than others."

"I don't trust myself enough."

"I wish he could just see what he's missing out on."

"An ingrained pattern of behavior, coping mechanisms, maybe I don't want to? Maybe I'm afraid to let go?"

"I don't know how to just accept myself for who I am. I don't know where to start."

"The only way I know how to numb these feelings is to use."

"Because I'm not out of the hole I've dug for myself yet."

"I'm afraid I'll relapse."

"I'm too lazy."

"My broken brain makes me self-conscious."

I'm not _____ enough.

There is no good excuse to hold on to your pain or cling to the obstacle. I don't know how to speak Latin, but it doesn't mean I can't learn. There are excuses not to, but none of them are acceptable. Stop letting your excuses hold you back. If you have made it this far, congratulations. You deserve everything. Now ask yourself the last two questions.

What is something I want to let go of?

Why haven't I let this go yet?

Change involves challenging what is most familiar to you. I believe what is most familiar, is your voice. It is the voice that will remind you (good and bad). It is the voice that will guide you. It is the voice that will speak to you most often. Are you willing to change the script you have been speaking? Have you already? Use your new script to guide you through your obstacle.

A muscle develops when it goes beyond its comfort level for an extended period of time. Practice. Repeat. Learn. Repeat. Fail. Repeat. Commit and continue.

In your written response to "Why haven't I let this go yet?" did you respond from the mind or from the heart? Did you already forget to go downstairs?

The written responses I included in this chapter, have been rehearsed over and over, dozen, hundreds, maybe thousands of times, internally and out loud. When things are repeated, they become your pattern. If you are going to interrupt your pattern, you must change your focus. In order to change, you must first acknowledge. Call out what is it that you want to alter by bringing it to your attention. Without awareness, there can be no action.

Focus on the things that excite you, that move you, that captivate you in a healthy manner. Focus on the things that empower you. Focus on the things that draw you in. Delete all things that weaken you (even if it's a person). Begin asking questions that will allow you access to the resources that are within you. The question, "Can I really do that?" is one born of doubt. "Why can't I get over what happened to me?" "Why can't I lose the weight?" "Why can't I stop the behavior?" In these questions, you are telling yourself something that cannot be done. You have already created a limitation on what you can do. You have built the wall that you cannot climb or disassemble. (In reality, you've told yourself you can't climb this wall. But of course, you can. If you created it, you can dismantle it).

Let's reframe these questions. "How can I make this thing happen more powerfully than I have ever dreamed of while having fun while I am doing it?" "How can I be more successful in my recovery?" "What strengths do I possess which allow me to overcome my obstacles?" "How can I better improve my ability to _____?" I do not know how these questions feel to you reading them, but I know how they feel typing writing them. I know how they feel when I read them aloud to an audience or group of people.

I heard Tony Robbins say something like, "There is no capability of difference in between you and someone you consider to be a role model of success." And it's true. They may have been born into a different socioeconomic class than you, but there is nothing they have that you do not that will allow or disallow you to obtain what you truly desire. Lack is a state of mind. All the scarcity in my life began in my own mind. All my limitations will first begin in my own mind. The things that you think are impossible or difficult are only that way because of the way you are focusing on these things- how they can't be done, not how they can, will and have already been done. If you focus on how things can't be done, they never will be. You have already overcome this situation in the past. If not the same, one very similar to it. Have you forgotten? Do you not remember how you went through this obstacle the last time? Will you envision yourself going through this in the future?

After you read each question, close your eyes and respond.

What are you most happy about in your life right now?

What about that makes you happy?

How does that make you feel? What does happiness really feel like to you? Allow yourself to feel this. Exist in this moment for as long as you will.

What else are you happy about in your life right now?

What about that makes you happy?

What are you excited about in your life right now?

What else?

What are you really grateful for in your life right now?

Do you notice a change in state (mental, emotional, spiritual, and physical) now that is different than what you felt before you started responding to these questions?

What are you really proud of in your life right now?

Who do you love the most in your life right now?

Who loves you the most in your life right now?

Think about it. Feel it. Bring it closer to you. Smell the air around this person.

Is there anyone in your life you would like to forgive right now?

Is that person you?

What would you want to say to this person?

What would you like them to know?

How would you like them to respond?

What if every morning, or every time you felt self-doubt, or every time you chose to become angered, agitated or frustrated, you began asking yourself a serious of custom-made questions that fostered a state of love, excitement, passion, and forgiveness? What is every time you felt negativity, you allowed yourself to experience feeling that would expand you? What would that do to the quality of your life? How would it improve your work? How would it improve your relationships? How would it improve your home life? How would it improve all of your experiences?

When you enter this state, you are more likely to go through the obstacle, than around it. In this state, you believe you are able to. The problem is not the situation that occurs to you, it is your response to the situation that occurs to you. You chose how you feel. The above questions are proof.

In this state, when you whisper the words, "I am enough," you believe.

Courage

"External factors influence the path, but not the
direction: forward."
-Ryan Holiday

Brene Brown stated, "Courage is showing up
without the certainty of outcome." This statement
does not mean showing up unprepared and risking it
all on a gamble. It is not a gamble at all. If you have
gotten this far in the book, if you have taken an
appropriate amount of time to tend to the internal
work these questions guided you to address, then
you are prepared. It is not luck. Luck isn't real.
Gambling is not fortune or misfortune. Every win
comes from someone else's loss. It is not planned,
and it is not earned.

I believe that I have accurately painted the picture
of how to move from the head to the heart. The goal
is to abide in the heart at all times; to allow love to
be in our major operating force, to be our drive and
our motivator. I speak with people almost daily that
discuss "finding motivation." People, who have no
motivation, feel they are not contributing. They are
not being productive and, in my experience,
overlook their strengths and qualities.

I spoke with a woman today and asked what her
strengths are. Her response, "I don't have any." She
also told me she wanted to be a social worker earlier
in our conversation. I inquired why she wanted to
be a social worker. She stated, "I want to help

people." I inquired, "Are you compassionate?"
"Yes," she replied. "Do you care about other
people? Do you believe you can impact others?"
Again, she responded, "Yes." I highlighted this
professional is not glamorous, there are losses, and
most people are not financially abundant in this
field. She stated awareness of all the things I
mentioned. It was not my intent to change her mind,
of course.

I then began to highlight her compassion, her sense
of being called to help the less fortunate, to give, to
care and to love others. All strengths. All within.
All overlooked. I asked her why she didn't list
these. She identified, "I don't feel like I'm good
enough." When someone else tells you how you
feel, you may fight it. You may disagree. When it
comes from within, organically and fluidly, you
respond differently. You have an open mind
regarding a previously hidden area. She was now
telling a stranger (me) that she felt she was not good
enough. "Of course, you are good enough. And you
have no proof otherwise," I said to her. She gently
smiled and wiped a tear from her eye. I didn't give
her any answer to a question. I didn't uncover some
mystery of the universe. I met her where she was. I
wasn't a life raft and I wasn't a safety net. I didn't
expect her to come to where I stand but found dry
land on her own- by listening to her heart and by
acknowledging the love that pours out of her. She

also said she didn't know how to love herself, but that she wanted to learn how.

It takes moments to open your heart and it takes moments to close your heart. When you are open, you are exposed and vulnerable. When you are open you will feel pain and disappointment. You will feel anxious and you will feel fear. However, you will also feel love and warmth. You will experience growth and expanse. You will experience peace only because you know what chaos feels like. You will know joy because you know turmoil.

When there is no enemy within, the enemy outside can do you no harm. You chose what you allow to affect you. You have the ability to choose a new viewpoint. You have every capability anyone else has to succeed, to love yourself, and to accept yourself in all of your beauty and limitations. If you can choose one thing to be passionate about in this world, choose you. You are worth being chosen first for the team. You are worth accepting nothing but the best. You are worth falling and crumbling and being rebuilt. The Liberty Bell is priceless because of its imperfection. Without it, it's just another bell. You are set apart because of your scars. It is time to embrace them courageously. Do not put off any longer what you have been avoiding. The "I will do it later" mentality allows you to remain stagnant. Later never comes. There is only now.

I recently asked numerous people to describe the most courageous thing they have ever done. The responses were:

"Admitting I'm an alcoholic."

"Getting honest."

"Going to treatment for my addiction."

"Getting a trade instead of graduating high school."

"Believing I am worth more."

"Allowing myself to feel uncomfortable."

"Saying no."

"Setting boundaries."

"Feeling emotions without using a substance to numb what I do not want to feel."

"Jumping out of an airplane."

"Saying 'I do.'"

"Bringing a child into the world."

"Getting a divorce."

"Developing my voice."

"Creating healthy and achievable expectations."

"Talking about traumas that occurred to me."

"Developing healthy friendships."

"Working on my codependency."

"Telling someone I was suicidal."

"Confronting my mother/father/spouse."

"Standing when I feel like running away."

"Addressing the issues I've been avoiding."

"Believing in myself."

"Believing in others."

What about you? What is the most courageous thing you have ever done? Write it below.

_____

_____

_____

_____

I then inquired, "What did you risk by being courageous?" The answers I got are as follows:

"My self-esteem."

"My job/career."

"My marriage."

"My friendships and reputation."

"My family."

"People would know my secrets."

"Other people would see my scars that I have kept hidden."

"My desire to keep using drugs."

"Getting out of my comfort zone."

"My unhealthy patterns."

"If I told someone, then I would have to do something about it."

"Giving up control."

"My pain and my excuses."

"I was being vulnerable and exposed."

"My shame and guilt."

"My identity."

"Feeling discomfort."

"Leaving the chaos, I don't know how to function without it."

Again, what about you? By being courageous, by going through your obstacle, what is at risk?

_____

_____

_____

_____

_____

_____

As people responded to me, I questioned if these things were really at risk or if there were self-created. A gentleman who replied his "career and reputation" were at stake went on to say, "Actually, being courageous was probably the thing that saved it. Everyone knew I was an alcoholic except me. But I really did know. I just didn't know what to do. Admitting I was scared and had a problem is what allowed the things I thought I was risking being saved." What a profound revelation. Another man stated, "By being honest I was risking my comfort zone. I was telling someone else things no one else knew. It was scary, but I've gained quite a bit of freedom just by opening up. It wasn't being honest with someone else that worried me, it was being honest with myself that I didn't want to do. I wanted to have reasons to justify the way I felt instead of doing anything about it. It took responsibility away from the other person and put it on me." Another lady stated, "Setting boundaries was very hard for me and I didn't want to do it. I've always avoided confrontations and conflicts, but after having a difficult discussion with some family members, I now feel happy, successful and accomplished."

As you are aware, it takes more than thinking yourself into happiness. It takes action. A simple action (investment) can lead to a profound result (return). The greater the investment, the greater the return.

These groups ended by me asking one last question for them to ruminate on. What would you have risked by not being courageous? What is at risk by not going through your obstacle? What lesson will you not learn if you do not continue forward? What potential understanding are you willing to trade for stagnation and decay?

By not being courageous, exposed, and vulnerable, what are you risking?

_____

_____

_____

_____

_____

_____

_____

_____

_____

_____

_____

_____

_____

_____

_____

_____

_____

_____

_____

I gave the first few chapters to a really good friend of mine with whom I worked. I saw work in past tense because she took the information that was presented and transformed her life and her desires. She was the first person at my current job that I allowed to know I was writing a book. I trust her as an equal and I value her input. About a month had passed and my mind (the upstairs) was telling me things like, "She isn't talking about it because it's not good," "Don't bring it up, she's doesn't' like it, you should try something else," and even "Don't try something else, no one wants to hear what you have to say. You aren't helping anyone." I allowed things to just play out naturally as opposed to being a "bother" (upstairs talk) and asking for input.

She was in my office one evening and she told me she was really doing the work in the book. I tried to not smile like a 7-year-old on Christmas, but I don't think I pulled it off. She told me that she was interested in working with children now as opposed to working with adult addicts. Quite the change. Quite the leap. Within weeks she had accepted a position, doing something completely different than she thought she would do for the rest of her life. Within weeks she was gone from the company, but very much present in Spirit. She has no idea of the impact on me that she has had. A few sentences really do not suffice.

Don't ever doubt your impact. Don't ever doubt your ability to make a change. You will never know how truly remarkable you are. You are no less Divine than the wind that blows the trees. Your heart will serve as your constant reminder if you allow it to speak.

YOUR MIND, THE DOCUMENTARY MAKER (self-as-context)

Have you ever watched a documentary on Africa? What did you see? Lots of crocodiles, lions, antelopes, gorillas, and giraffes? Tribal dances? Military conflict? Political upheaval? Colorful marketplaces? Amazing mountains? Beautiful, calm villages in the countryside? Poverty-stricken slums? Starving children? You can learn a lot from watching a documentary, but one thing is for sure: a documentary about Africa is not Africa itself.

A documentary can give you impressions of Africa. It can certainly show you some dramatic sights and sounds. But it wouldn't even come close to the actual experience of traveling there in the flesh. No matter how brilliantly filmed, no matter how "authentic" it is, a documentary about Africa is not the same thing as Africa itself.

Similarly, a documentary about you would not be the same thing as you yourself. Even if that documentary lasted for a thousand hours and included all sorts of relevant scenes from your life, all sorts of interviews with people who know you, and all sorts of fascinating details about your innermost secrets, even then the documentary would not be you.

To really clarify this, think of the person you love most on this planet. Now, which would you prefer to spend time with: the actual living person or a documentary about that person?

So, there's this huge difference between who we are and any documentary that anyone could ever make about us—no matter how "truthful" that documentary may be. And I've put "truthful" in quotation marks because all documentaries are hopelessly biased in that they only show you a tiny part of the big picture. Since the advent of cheap video, the typical hour-long TV documentary is the "best" of literally dozens, if not hundreds of hours of footage. So inevitably it's going to be quite biased.

And the bias of a human film director is nothing compared to the bias of our thinking self. Out of an entire lifetime of experience—literally hundreds of thousands of hours of archival film footage- our thinking self selects a few dramatic memories, edits them together with some related judgments and opinions, and turns it into a powerful documentary, entitled "This Is Who I Am!"

And the problem is, when we watch that documentary, we forget that it's just a heavily edited video. Instead, we believe that we are that video. But in the same way that a documentary about Africa is not Africa, a documentary of you is not you.

(Reading exercise from Acceptance Commitment Therapy).

Lasting change involves redefining your standards. The common denominator in all the things you have achieved thus far is that you believed you must achieve these things. You did not settle, and you did not compromise. People tend to not take seriously things they "should" do. We all know we should eat differently, should exercise differently, should communicate differently, should love differently, but it is when you "must" do these things that they are attained. It's a New Year's Resolution otherwise. If you choose to wait until New Years to make a change, it's not important enough for it to stick. Knowing smoking is harmful isn't enough to quit. Lung cancer, however, is. Pain is an excellent motivator. Do you want to wait until the obstacle is farther out of reach to begin reaching out for it? Or will you reach from where you are? You have every capability to be successful. You are no different, worse off, or better off than any other person trying to accomplish the same goal you are. Make a real resolution, today. Continue the resolution you made yesterday and the day before. Shift your shoulds to musts then redefine your standards. Recreate the documentary you watch repeatedly. Rewrite the script that you speak to yourself. You will act consistently with who you believe yourself to be. If you define yourself as broken, you will act as though you are broken. If you define yourself as too tired, then you will not believe yourself to be able to achieve that which you want to obtain. Are you acting on a set of beliefs that you made months, years, or even decades ago? Were these beliefs handed to you or perhaps even forced onto you?

Les Brown said, "Most people don't fail in life because they aim too high and miss. People fail in life because they aim too low and hit."

When you raise your standards, you will find that you are no longer settling for the mundane and monotony.

How long are you able to tread water? Answer honestly before looking at the next question.

What if you were capsized in the ocean? How long would you be able to tread water?

I have no doubt that you answered these two questions differently. Your ability did not change. Your muscle tone stayed the same. Your conditioning remained as is current.

What changed? (Your belief system. Nothing more.)

What else are you not doing because you are telling yourself you can't? What have you put off because you tell yourself you *should* do it instead of *must* do it? What is on your to-do list that you keep pushing off to later? The future is only now. The future only exists in the present tense. Be here now. Commit to your expansion.

You are more than you have believed yourself to be. Say it out loud with me:

I am enough.

I have always been enough.

I will always be enough.

The final guided meditation is to sit in nature or any other environment of your choosing and reflect on what it truly means, to you, to be enough. Stay here, in these sacred moments, as long as you will allow yourself to be still. Stay one moment longer each day until you lose the desire to track time. After all, you are worth everything.

Chapter Thirteen

For the first year this book was available, this chapter was not included. What is written on the next few pages is about (the continuation of) bringing love to ourselves, but also extending it to others. The purpose of I Am Enough is to develop a love for the self. One cannot give away what one does not have. If you have made it this far, then you have put in time and effort to look deep within and begin an internal healing process- the healing that one must do on their own accord. "Chapter Thirteen" is the process of extending love to others. It is the first step in healing our outside relationships. First to me, then to you. This is the way in which love must be given. Most of us get this backward. Here is my take on bringing help to others...

If we are to help our loved ones, we have to love our loved ones. Do we really understand love? Is it conditioned? Is it one-sided? Are there boundaries? Is it always calm or soothing? Is it always tough? Is it extended but then revoked when a "bad deed" is committed? Do we fully understand love?

Love is patient. Am I giving others the same room to make mistakes as I want them to give me? Do I offer forgiveness and room for growth, the same way in which I need forgiveness and room for growth? Do I know that other are fallible human beings, just the same as I am? Or, if I offer patient love to others, do I in turn offer it to myself? Do I have a belief that "I am different" and therefore undeserving of this quality of self-love? Do I allow others to err and then beat myself up when I make a mistake?

Love is kind. Do the people I love actually enjoy being around me? Take a moment and ask yourself-Do the people I love the most practice being in my presence, or do they avoid me? If someone around me falls, do I point out the obstacle, or do I offer a hand? Do I say, "I told you," or "you should have listened to me?" Do I come off as arrogant or do I come off as gentle? Do I enjoy being around me? If I were to sit in a quieted room, with just my thoughts, what would they speak to me? Are the thoughts I have about myself nurturing or neglecting?

Love always protects. Do I have my loved one's back? Do I believe in them? Do I show it? Do I demand loyalty without giving it? If my loved one falls, do they come to me for help? Are they honest with me? Do I support them? Do they feel safe around me? Do I feel safe around me? Do I show support for myself? Do I defend myself when others speak ill of me, or do I apologize even when I've done no wrong to another? Would I go to me when I needed help?

Love always trusts. Trust is earned. Of this I am fully aware. Do I believe in others abilities or do I remind them of their scars? Do I point out their strengths, or do I remind them of their failures? Am I encouraging? When we interact, do others leave feeling wanted and welcomed? Do I remind myself of my scars and negate my own beauty? Do I believe in myself and know I am capable of all things? If I were to speak to other the way I speak to myself, would there be an audience?

Love always hopes. Do I automatically assume the worst about my loved one? Am I letting the past cloud the present? Am I letting fear/anxiety predict the future? Does my loved one know fully that I am on their side? Does my loved one know completely that I believe in them? Am I letting my past get in the way of today? Am I expecting the worse and preparing for the least? Am I in my own corner? If my expectations were written out on paper for others to view, would anyone want to read them?

Love always perseveres. Am I quick to give up on my loved one after they make a mistake? Am I willing to love them through it if they do? If they fall, do I remind them of their bruises or their beauty? Have I given up on myself? Am I willing to get up and do for myself what only I can do even when I don't feel motivated? If I don't like the way I look, am I willing to change it? If so, to what extent? If my thoughts don't sustain me, am I willing to create new ones? Am I willing to treat myself better than any other has treated me? Am I willing to do this for another?

<u>Love never fails</u>. People will not remember us for what we accomplish. They will remember how we made them feel and what we helped them to accomplish. This is true leadership. This is true compassion. This is the unconditioned love that we fail giving to others, and we fail giving to ourselves. To what cost are you willing to alter the way things have been done, by you and to you? Seeing your extreme worth is a choice.

What is the message I am giving to others? Am I coming off as critical or encouraging? Is my message one of hope or one of doubt? Am I feeding into fear or feeding into faith?

Are you more interested in what your loved one is doing or what they are becoming?

Have you been more interested in what you are doing than what you are becoming?

Made in the USA
Las Vegas, NV
15 October 2021